"This book is at the same time a Bible study a~~~~ journey into the 'more' of God. If you have pursuing the presence of God and the outbreak of His Kingdom on earth, this book will help you. If you are on that journey but have questions, this book will help you. Pete is a man of real courage. He lives this stuff and so does his exciting church. They are supernatural; they take the intervention of the unseen into the seen seriously. Big thanks to you, Pete and Kim, and all at NKCC, for becoming a great help and hope to many others who are seeking to embrace more of heaven on earth in these days."

> Andy Merrick, elder, Hope Church, Glasgow;
> www.hopechurchglasgow.org

"God is doing wonderful things in our day that make us hungry to be transformed by the renewing of our minds. This book will make the process easier. Pete highlights a few things that were clearly visible in the life of Jesus (grace, sonship, freedom . . .) that they may become so in ours, too. Let's 'unwrap' everything that gets in the way of this! Because these truths are demonstrated in his own life, Pete is able to talk about them in a way that is both engaging and full of real wisdom."

> Jean Hay, elder, Assemblée Chrétienne Alès Cévennes; www.ac-ac.fr

"The story of God at work is a very simple and down-to-earth business. In *Unwrapping Lazarus*, Pete gives us his insights into how biblical transformation is taking place in our world today."

> Joel Edwards, director, Micah Challenge International;
> chair, EXPOSED, www.exposed2013.com

"With apostolic insight, penetrating analysis and practical examples from life, work and ministry, Pete Carter invites us to examine our preconceptions about the Kingdom and the Church. As he unwraps the death clothes of Lazarus for us, we will want to shed our unhelpful traditions, false humility and lingering legalism and embrace freedom, royal sonship and the new wine of the Holy Spirit.

"I have had the great privilege of working closely with Pete in the NKCC leadership team and seeing firsthand his love, compassion, wisdom, faith and, most of all, his passion for the presence of God. Pete's book will provoke your thinking and, if you need it, rattle your cage. You will discover more of the goodness of God, the power of the cross and faith to see signs and wonders. You will be empowered to develop a naturally supernatural lifestyle. You will find revelation and stimulus to increase the manifestation of heaven on earth."

David Webster, senior leader and director,
NKCC Schools of Supernatural Ministry

"In *Unwrapping Lazarus*, Dr. Pete Carter will take you on an adventure. He is a man who is hungry for more of Jesus. He knows his Bible, loves the Church and is living a righteous life. Nonetheless, he hungers for more of the abundant life he's heard so much about. This book is not only about his own personal transformation in his relationship with Jesus, it is also a map for all who desire to accept the invitation from heaven to believe for more than you have ever considered before. In these pages are enough courage, risk and revelation to spark a personal revival for the reader and a corporate revival for those who hear the testimonies. If you want to realize the promises of Scripture and see heaven made manifest in your life, then I highly recommend that you read this book and that you prepare yourself for an encounter with the living God."

Danny Silk, director, Global Transformation Institute;
senior management team, Bethel Church, Redding, California

"In this dynamic book, Pete Carter has beautifully interwoven tremendous apostolic insights and understanding with real-life examples and testimonies to give us an incredibly interesting, challenging and edifying result. Pete is a well-respected medical doctor who was divinely shifted into apostolic and pastoral ministry. The insights he shares about his journey and of Lazarus are powerful truths that Pete has paid a great price to obtain and convey. This book will give you hope and encouragement for taking off the clothes of your history and lifeless religion, while also creating an appetite for the liberty and fullness of the Holy Spirit God has for you as His much-loved child."

Dr. Michael Maiden, lead pastor, Church for the Nations,
Phoenix, Arizona; president, Church on the Rock International

"*I like that guy!* was my concluding thought after spending a day with Pete Carter. What I enjoyed most was my talk with him about what God is doing today. I found his insights full of revelation that feed my spirit. *Unwrapping Lazarus* will help you see areas where adjustment is needed so that your Christian life can be more fulfilling. It is a must-read book for today's Christian. Taking time to read this book will be well worth it."

Dr. Roberts Liardon, Roberts Liardon Ministries;
author, *God's Generals* book series

# UNWRAPPING
# LAZARUS

# UNWRAPPING
# LAZARUS

*Freeing the
Supernatural in Your Life*

## PETE CARTER

**Chosen**

*a division of Baker Publishing Group*
Minneapolis, Minnesota

Published by Chosen Books
11400 Hampshire Avenue South
Bloomington, Minnesota 55438
www.chosenbooks.com

Chosen Books is a division of
Baker Publishing Group, Grand Rapids, Michigan

Printed in the United States of America

Library of Congress Cataloging-in-Publication Data is on file at the Library of Congress, Washington, DC.

ISBN 978-0-8007-9583-2 (pbk.)

Cover design by Dual Identity

14   15   16   17   18   19   20        7   6   5   4   3   2   1

# CONTENTS

# CONTENTS

# FOREWORD

I am always impressed by people who are quite established in their ministries or careers who come to a place like Bethel Church in Redding, California, to learn as though they were novices. It is humbling, actually. Often these are the ones who are already great leaders in their spheres of influence and have a significant following of their God-given gift and ability. Yet they come for weeks, and sometimes months, just to glean from the wonderful presence of God among us. Such is the case with Pete and Kim Carter. They came, not as experts but as hungry believers.

We welcomed them as a part of the family . . . our tribe. They had access to various members of our team and joined us for staff meetings, etc. It was a great joy for us, as I believe it was for them. The outcome is a friendship that easily spans distance and time to form a partnership for Kingdom exploits.

While this book is truly Pete Carter's "material," it is consistent with the mandate that we all feel is necessary for the Church in this hour. Not only that, but our friendship is a practical example of the partnership that we are feeling is necessary between the Church of the United Kingdom and the Church of the United States. It seems to be an essential heavenly mandate upon these two nations that will benefit us both, but more importantly will enable us to have impact on the nations of the world much more effectively.

*Unwrapping Lazarus* is a wonderful book that is both inspired instruction and a written record of a journey. And I can't think of a better combination. The journey is that of this marvelous couple, Pete and Kim Carter. Pete made a dramatic adjustment in careers, joining to his stance as a respected doctor the additional position of pastor and church leader in the U.K. His unusual combination of both ministry and medical experience affords him insights that would be hard to come by any other way. I love how he weaves the experiences from these two distinct professions into a beautiful tapestry revealing what freedom really looks like, thus the title *Unwrapping Lazarus*.

We are citizens of a Kingdom known by freedom. The presence of the Spirit of God in our lives is unto that purpose—liberty! But the more profound journey as recorded in this book is much more than a change in professions. It is a shift in mindsets that affects every profession and discipline. Simply put, it is a change from a traditional, acceptable view of life to a true Kingdom perspective of life. What this statement lacks in profundity, it more than makes up for in the revolutionary nature of its impact. This is the kind of change that inspires a shift in the culture we live in. And that by itself is transformational in nature.

Much like a doctor performing surgery, the author exposes and removes the roots in our thinking that keep us from the freedoms we were actually born for. But also much like a doctor, Pete tenderly cares for the reader in a way that communicates that this is a grace work, not a "you must work harder to fulfill God's purposes in your life" work. That, in itself, is refreshing.

I believe the impact of *Unwrapping Lazarus* will be powerful and long lasting. It needs to be read by people from a great variety of backgrounds and occupations, as these truths apply to everyone. We were born for the freedom described on these pages. Be ready to be inspired, instructed and encouraged.

Bill Johnson, senior leader, Bethel Church, Redding, California; author, *When Heaven Invades Earth*, and co-author, *The Essential Guide to Healing*

# ACKNOWLEDGMENTS

There are so many people who have affected my life and contributed to the writing of this book that it would be impossible to mention them all. However, thanks to you all anyway.

One person has accompanied me on my journey of life in a way that no one else ever could. We have laughed together, cried together, dreamed together and had more fun and adventures over the last 35 years than I could have imagined possible at the beginning. Her name is Kim, my beautiful wife—thank you for such an amazing life together. This book is also your story. I love you more and more.

Our children, David and Kerry, have brought such joy to my life. This book would not have been complete without the contribution of your lives. My life is continually enriched by yours.

Thank you, Jo, for becoming part of the Carter family and joining in the fun and adventure.

Zoe and Samuel—you are wonderful gifts to us. I so enjoy my granddad times with you.

To my sister, Christine, thanks for spurring your little brother on.

To North Kent Community Church—for me personally the most amazing church family in the world. Thanks for letting me be me. I love living my life among you.

Also to my friends at the church in Ales, south of France—thank you for walking alongside us on our journey of faith.

To Bethel Church in Redding, California, and all our friends there—thank you for opening your hearts and arms to us, loving us and becoming friends. Thank you for being pioneers in the faith and opening doors so that others may follow.

To Ray Lowe for your friendship, and for helping me know how to live in the grace of God.

Lastly, to Mum and Dad: You enabled me to dream big things and have the courage to attempt them, and you gave me an amazing foundation for life. As I have discovered more about the Father heart of God, I have realized in even greater measure what wonderful parents I have.

Thank you all for helping to form me and form this book.

# 1

# UNWRAPPING IMPOSSIBILITY

## *Revealing the Reality of Miracles*

His name was Otilio. He was an indigenous Mexican of the Pame tribe, and he lived in the central part of Mexico in a remote mountain village. He was eighteen years old and was about to transform his area and his tribe, although he had no idea that was his destiny.

It was 1995, and since the age of eight he had been paralyzed in all four limbs after being beaten up by some other children, who also assaulted his head mercilessly with rocks, leaving him severely brain damaged. His mother tried to look after him as best she could. She was small and frail and her countenance was understandably sad. There were no other children to be seen, and as far as I could ascertain, the father had abandoned the family.

"Home" consisted of a hut constructed by putting sticks next to each other in the ground; the roof was fashioned from various odds and ends. There was nothing between the sticks to keep out the wind and cold, inescapable conditions of their mountainous winter. The floor was compacted mud, and an open fireplace on the floor, with a few sticks of wood, served as her cooking stove. It was a desolate picture, occasionally brightened when some men from the village would come to carry Otilio outside to lie in the sunshine for a few hours. Other than that, Otilio lay on a bed made of woven reeds with a small threadbare blanket to cover him and just his mother to care for him.

I looked at his poor body, little more than skin and bones, and felt useless in my capacity as a medical doctor. The local people had raised their hopes at the news of my coming and were wondering what miracles this British doctor could do with his education and experience. Such hopes raised simply by my presence became quite a burden, but even in the best hospitals in England the outlook would have been bleak. Here, with no medical facilities at all, I could not see how I could help as a doctor.

We had traveled to the region to offer support to an exceptional young couple, Pepe and Vero, who were missionaries living there trying to bring hope to a people who were downcast and downtrodden. Dysentery was rife because of the polluted drinking water taken from the local rivers. There was no clean water supply. It was a familiar sight to see donkeys laden with water containers being driven reluctantly the few miles backward and forward to the river.

It had been a long journey, ten hours' drive from Leon, the last two and a half hours on unmade mountain roads that barely merited the title. There were nine of us in the van, plus the family dog of the couple who were driving us there. This trip to Mexico was the first time Andy Merrick and I had met; it would prove to be the start of a lasting friendship. Fortunately for me, Andy was sitting next to the dog! A few hours into our journey, we realized that a good number of other passengers had hitched a ride on the dog—passengers of the jumping, biting kind. It was difficult not to scratch.

When we arrived at our destination we were very happy to get out of the van. We were introduced to Pepe and Vero, who greeted us with warm smiles and offered us something to drink. Pepe is a bit of a genius when it comes to innovation, and his ingenuity was most helpful in that remote place. He had rigged up a system whereby a container of water would get heated by the sun during the day, so that a warm shower was possible. Such pleasantries are taken so much for granted by those of us who live in many other parts of the world.

That night four of us bedded down in the chapel, sleeping bags on pews, balancing carefully so as not to fall off and end up on the floor with the scorpions and black widow spiders. There was no electricity once the generator was turned off; it was pitch black. I was amazed by the noise generated in such a remote place—donkeys, dogs, cockerels, pigs and chickens all seemed to think that darkness was a sign for the ultimate sing-along. As I lay there in the darkness, I wondered what lay ahead of us in the next few days, prayed for God to do amazing things and eventually drifted off to sleep.

The next morning we awoke to more pitch blackness—the shutters on the windows effectively blocking any light. We used our flashlights to check around us for anything nasty, banged our shoes out in case any scorpions had taken refuge in them and, having decided all was clear, ventured to our feet and opened the shutters. We were greeted by a beautiful sight: mountains, trees and blue sky. I felt ready for the day ahead. The call of nature took me to the not-so-pleasant long-drop toilet, which I was glad to escape from.

Breakfast was not ready yet, so I decided to go for a stroll in the village, walking along the mountain roads trying to get a feel for the environment and praying as I went. Generally speaking, the Pame as a tribe are short in stature, and I am reasonably tall, so greeting eye to eye was a slight challenge. As I walked along, I met several local people and tried a greeting of *Buenos dias*, hoping that they could understand my rather poor Spanish. I realized that some of them spoke only the local Pame language, but I thought that they would acknowledge me at least. After a few attempts I was rather baffled, as my greetings seemed to fall on deaf ears. The people shuffled past me awkwardly, not even raising their heads to look at me, but rather lowering their heads further and looking at the ground. Surely my Spanish was not that bad! Did they not recognize my greeting?

As I continued this walk, and in the days ahead, I came to learn that these people lived under a cloud of shame, a lack of dignity and hopelessness. They obviously felt inferior and unable to connect with this white stranger.

I learned of their history of retreat from conquistadors centuries ago, retreat that had finally deposited them in this inhospitable place. They were victims of a cruel world, downtrodden and hopeless, fatalistic in their attitude, accepting of the harshness of life. This was evident in even the most basic decisions—starting with the water they drank. Despite various attempts to educate them on the importance of boiling the water drawn from the river before they drank it, they ignored the advice, preferring to trust to fate. The result was that about a quarter of their children died before the age of five from amoebic dysentery. Such misery and sadness was part of life itself.

But that was about to change as God did what only He can do.

## Will God's Power Work Through Me?

I returned to Pepe and Vero's hut thinking of breakfast. We had brought most of our supplies with us, since the nine of us would overload the local system, and it was about a three-hour drive to a town where food could be purchased. We chatted and decided that, after breakfast, we would set off to visit various sick people scattered around the small settlements in the mountains.

Thus, before long, we found ourselves squeezing back into the van. Including Pepe and Vero there were now eleven of us, plus the dog and his little companions. We bumped along the road until we came to a large settlement where we parked the van and set off on foot. It was a warm day and we were at quite an altitude, so the walking was strenuous. After about half an hour we came to a small settlement consisting of a few huts. There were one or two women to be seen.

Pepe and Vero had been visiting this village regularly and knew the way to the hut where Otilio lay. As we approached, a small woman appeared, head bowed down, shoulders stooped, a frail hand offered limply in greeting. She led the way into the hut. Inside was dim and my eyes adjusted slowly to the light level.

Lying motionless on a thin reed mat, which was his bed, was Otilio, a threadbare blanket draped over the skin and bones that made his body. His mother stood to one side and let me pass. I had no idea what was going through her mind as this doctor from some faraway country entered her home in order to help her son. My heart was stirred with compassion as I regarded this scene of utter poverty. Never had I seen such a desolate sight. Yet somehow, hope was being placed in me.

I went over and examined Otilio as best I could in the circumstances, quickly ascertaining that he had a spastic paralysis of all four limbs and that his mental function was also impaired. I looked at him and he looked at me, both of us uncomprehending that this was a day of extraordinary significance. I felt helpless; there was no hope medically, but hope stirred within me as the God of hope whispered to me, *You can pray.*

As a Christian, I knew this already, of course. And, of course, I was planning to pray, but an invitation from God Himself put a different light on it. I was willing to pray, but was I willing to hope that something was going to happen? In my experience, I had sometimes prayed out of Christian duty without much hope of change, but here that did not seem an option. Was I willing to risk praying with the expectation of something happening to Otilio? Was I willing to risk disappointment if nothing happened?

The rest of the party seemed to be waiting for my lead, so I explained briefly my assessment of the situation and said that we were going to pray for Otilio. Through translation we asked for his mother's permission to pray for him and lay hands on him. She agreed without any sense of anticipation. I knelt down, placed my hands on Otilio's fragile frame and started to ask the God of miracles to do a miracle.

As we prayed, I heard God whisper to me, *Ask to lift his blanket off him*. This seemed like a simple request. I asked and the mother agreed. Now we could see his body in more detail—his legs constantly in spasm, "scissored" across each other; his arms bent across his upper body, a twisted form. We continued to pray and my heart was stirred even more.

Fortunately, I was praying with my eyes open, because as we prayed I noticed Otilio's arms and legs relax and go floppy—still paralyzed, but with a different form known as flaccid paralysis. I moved one of his legs and it moved easily rather than jerking with the spasms. Something was happening to Otilio. My medical training was proving to be of use after all: I could see this sign of God's activity that the others were unaware of. (This underlines my belief that Christians with medical knowledge should be at the forefront of Christian healing, but that is for another time.)

God whispered to me again, *I want you to lift him up off his bed*. This was not such a simple assignment!

Two weeks previously, I had been at a conference in England—a gathering of church leaders—and we had been fortunate enough to have John and Carol Arnott, founding pastors of Catch the Fire (formerly the Toronto Airport Christian Fellowship), with us. They had prayed for me with a particular view to my upcoming trip to the Pame in Mexico. They had laid hands on me, one at my head, the other at my feet, and for about twenty minutes the power of God hit me and surged through my body like electricity. At times I felt that I might die, but I knew I would not. I wanted them to stop, but then again I did not. At the end I lay on the floor exhausted, knowing that I had encountered God in an awesome way. He had placed His power within me.

Back with Otilio, I had to face the question in my head: *Did I believe God's power would work through me to perform a miracle?* This was a large "leap of faith" if ever there had been one in my life. But I had heard God's invitation, so I turned to my colleagues, told them what I had noticed God already doing and what He had told me to do next.

I was hoping for some encouragement from the group. Another church leader from England was there with us, and to my shock he told me clearly that I could not lift Otilio off the bed. He was adamant. (Later I learned that he had a sister with a degree of paralysis who had not been healed despite much prayer. I guess he was not prepared to face possible disappointment.) I had a choice to make: Give in to the fear of disappointment or have faith in the power of God. The others, including Andy, made more encouraging noises. I decided to take the lead in the situation. I asked Otilio's mother if I could pick him up off his bed. She nodded her agreement.

Could I do this? With my heart thumping and my mind racing, I bent down and lifted Otilio from his bed. There was nothing of him; I could feel his bones, and as our eyes met, I seem to remember smiling at him while he gazed back at me. I guess he was wondering what was happening. Then I tipped his body so that his feet approached the ground, and once they touched, I let him go!

Immediately he stood and walked out of that hut for the first time in ten years, his muscles and coordination restored in an instant. Stunned, I followed him out into the sunshine, and I will forever remember when he lifted his head to look at the sky and smiled the most magnificent smile I have ever seen. He carried on his walk, exploring his environment. Our group was in tears, hugging one another, jumping up and down and marveling at the love and power of God. Otilio's mum followed us out of the hut. Her shoulders straightened, and her head came up.

God had started to heal a nation.

After a while we left Otilio and his mother. They could now enter into a new place of freedom from the affliction that had dominated their lives for the past ten years. There was a swing to our stride and a song in our hearts. I felt ready for anything. I do not remember the rest of the morning, but the afternoon and evening are etched upon my memory. If I thought the morning had been amazing, then God was preparing a lesson for me that was going to change me on an even deeper level.

## The Heart of the Matter

Back at the main village where Pepe and Vero lived, we set up a makeshift medical clinic. They had received, over the course of time, unwanted medicines donated by individuals and pharmacies with the thought that these might be useful to the Pame people. There were mounds of plastic bags on the floor of the hut in which Pepe and Vero lived, filled with all sorts of drugs. If I had wanted to perform a kidney transplant, I would have had the medication available for care afterward. I was reasonably certain, however, that I would not be entering into that level of expertise! I looked through the bags and pulled out the few basic drugs that would be useful, mainly antibiotics to try and counter the amoebic dysentery so common there.

News had obviously spread that a doctor was in the area and soon a long queue snaked back from the hut from which I was working. Old and young came. I tried to help people as quickly as I could, constantly aware of the large number of people waiting patiently, but was slowed because of having to work through a translator. I asked the others with me to pray for the people as they waited, and we prayed for each person I worked with.

Time passed and we were doing quite well. Then a mother arrived at the front of the queue. She was carrying her young daughter, who was about eighteen months old. I could see immediately that another miracle was needed. The poor child was suffering from dysentery and was already dehydrated. She was limp and her eyes were sunken back in their sockets; her skin had lost its elasticity and her pulse was rapid. If I had been back in England I would have immediately admitted her into a hospital, where intravenous fluids, antibiotics and full supportive care would probably have guaranteed a happy outcome. But that was not available here. I was not even confident that anything she drank to try to rehydrate her would not be contaminated by those wretched amoebae. I was also aware that she was probably beyond the point where drinking alone could rehydrate her sufficiently. I was so frustrated. I knew how to save her life, but the facilities were not available.

We had, however, already seen an amazing miracle that day; surely it was time for another. We started to pray, fully expecting to see the child recover in front of our eyes. But that did not happen. We continued to pray but nothing seemed to change.

How could this be? Pressure mounted as nothing happened and time passed. There was still a large queue of people waiting to see me, so reluctantly, I agreed that we needed to stop praying for this child and carry on seeing the rest of the people. We gave the mother the appropriate antibiotics, but I knew they would not work quickly enough; the child was nearing the point of no return.

As the mother walked away, cradling her daughter in her arms, I said to the people around me that the child was going to die and probably before the day was out. I struggled to understand and keep my emotions in check. Being a "true professional" I was able to put my feelings aside and carry on with my work. But my mind kept returning to that little girl.

Eventually, everyone was seen and most seemed content that they had visited the doctor. We stored the plastic bags back in the hut, and I put away my stethoscope and other medical equipment. We went inside for a meal, which was very welcome after a long day. That evening we were holding a meeting in the chapel with worship, Bible teaching and praying for the sick, and I was the guest speaker. I was happy to try to help these people in any way I could, and telling people about Jesus is the best news that I know. If they would enter into their own relationships with God through the Good News of Jesus, then they could start to discover for themselves all the resources of God available to them in their situations. I was excited to share this Good News.

It was dark inside the chapel, the small electricity generator just able to help two or three bulbs pierce the darkness. The worship was moving, as Pepe led us on his guitar. A number of locals joined in, but many remained quiet and subdued. I preached a message that seemed to stir people's hearts, although it was difficult to tell as I was unable to see most of their faces because of the lack of light. I concluded my message and said that we would be happy to pray for anyone who was sick so that they could be healed. Just as I finished this confident proclamation my heart sank.

My eyes had immediately fallen upon the mother of the young girl whom we had been unable to help that afternoon. There, lying across her lap in a lifeless form, was the little girl. I walked across the small dark space, trying to stir my faith. I talked to myself: *This morning you saw an amazing miracle; you can do it again.* Strengthened by such thoughts, I knelt down at the mother's side to examine the little one. She lay still, eyes rolled back in their sockets and unmoving. Her body was floppy and unresponsive. I tried to find a pulse without success. I tried to stimulate her into some sort of reaction, but all to no avail. About twice per minute a small gasp exited from her lips. Cheyne-Stokes breathing, or the death rattle as it is sometimes called, indicated imminent death. She was literally dying in front of our eyes; any breath could be her last.

I summoned the people with me to prayer, with a sort of confidence that seemed to encourage them. We called on the God of miracles to do it once again, only this time we needed to see resurrection not just healing. About twenty minutes passed, and I kept checking to see whether there was any change or indeed if she had actually stopped breathing. There was no improvement and each breath threatened to be the final call. I became angry with God. How could He not answer my prayers? How could He perform a miracle in the morning and allow this child to die in the evening? I prayed with more fervor, demanding a miracle from God—no change. I prayed some more, my emotions starting to boil over into my prayers.

After about thirty minutes I lost all control of my emotions and, giving up, walked away. My anger toward God spilled out. "Why, why, why?" I asked Him. I had no idea what other people around me were thinking; I was not sure I even cared.

As I ran out of things to say to God, He asked me a question: *Why are you praying?*

I thought that was obvious, but suddenly revelation entered my consciousness. Since that morning I had been rehearsing in my mind how to tell the story of Otilio once I got back home, thinking how impressed people would be, how my reputation in the Christian community would rise. I realized that I was not really praying for the benefit of the young girl and her mother; I was praying for my own benefit, to have another story to tell, to look more impressive in other people's sight. Love was not motivating my prayers, but rather power and influence. I started to cry at the realization, and I repented, telling God how sorry I was and how desperate I felt, somehow feeling responsible for this little girl's death.

Then something unexpected happened, something that I had never felt or experienced before, something that would change my life. The Holy Spirit poured Himself into me. I felt warmth and overwhelming love. The compassion of God flooded into my being. It was as if God broke off a bit of His heart and gave it to me. All of a sudden I loved that young girl with an unshakeable love. I cared for her in a way that compared to the way I feel about my own wife and children. I wanted her to live, and I did not care if I never got to tell the story. But surely it was too late.

The voice of God came to me once more, *Go to her again and ask the mother to put the child to her breast.* I walked back to the mother's side, understanding in a completely new way that love "always hopes" (1 Corinthians 13:7). Hope stirred in me, and with compassion and authority I asked the mother to put the child to her breast. She looked at me as if I were crazy, but she did what I asked. She lifted the girl's head toward her breast and let it go, and the lifeless body slumped back over her lap.

"Please, do it again," I asked and the mother complied. She put her hand behind her daughter's head and lifted her to the breast, and the girl started to suck, at first slowly, then hungrily. I stood back, amazed at the love and power of God in action. Ten minutes later the little girl was sitting normally on the mother's knee, full of life, looking around her, unaware that she was the center of attention and the cause for much rejoicing.

I walked away, thankful to God. I do not think I prayed for anyone else that night—I cannot really remember. My thoughts were filled with wonder at God and love for a young girl whose name I never knew.

The next couple of days passed happily, and then we left the Pame to return to a different life. Pepe and Vero remained there doing an amazing work, telling people about Jesus, establishing a church, bringing initiatives and generally enriching the lives of those around them. News about Otilio and the young girl circulated through the small mountain communities. Hope was stirring.

Almost exactly one year later, I had the privilege of returning to the Pame. The journey was much the same in length and comfort, minus a few little companions, but the sense of expectation was different—what would we find?

Once again we slept in the chapel and arose early the next day. I took myself off for a walk along the mountain paths. As I went I greeted people with *Buenos dias* and I noticed something that thrilled my heart—the people walked with their heads up, looked me in the eye and, with smiles, greeted me. The sense of shame and hopelessness had been shed like old rags, replaced by clothing of dignity and purpose.

Over the course of a year, the hope that had been born in them was bearing fruit. They were not a forgotten people; they were a people precious to God, among whom God had demonstrated His love and power. They were a nation changed. Since that time things have progressed further: Fresh water and electricity are available, decent houses are being constructed. The Pame are no longer a forgotten, downtrodden people.

Can miracles happen? Yes. I have seen them with my own eyes.

As I am writing this chapter, my mind has wandered back over the years of my Christian life, starting from when I was sixteen years old and God entered my life in an amazing way. At that age, I became spiritually alive and aware of the love and power of God.

I was restricted, however, by ways of thinking and behavior that somehow constrained the full expression of the life of God within me and through me. Like Lazarus when he was raised from the dead, but still restricted by his grave clothes, I needed to be unwrapped in order to live in the full potential of my Christian life.

Throughout this book I will share some of my life's journey and experiences, an exciting journey that continues to stimulate and excite me. I will talk about some of the major themes that have shaped my thinking—themes such as identity, unfolding revelation, the Kingdom of heaven, freedom, authority and wisdom. I hope that this book will help you to enjoy in greater measure the amazing abundance of the life that God has given you.

# 2

# UNWRAPPING LAZARUS

## Revealing the Fullness of New Life

His name was Lazarus.

He lived in Israel almost two thousand years ago. His hometown was Bethany, and he had two sisters, Martha and Mary. They were friends of Jesus; in fact, the Bible says that they were close friends and He loved them. John's gospel, in chapter 11, tells an amazing story involving this family that had a profound effect upon everyone involved—indeed upon every believer seeking to enter a new life of freedom and wholeness.

If you have read the gospel of John you are probably familiar with the story. And even if you have not read it, you are likely to be aware of it, because the name *Lazarus* has come to be associated with a miraculous return to life. This story is told generation after generation—powerful evidence of Jesus, the giver of life.

But it is possible to fail to see its astonishing application for each believer today. Beyond showing us who Jesus is, this story is showing us something about who we are.

One of the problems we have with grasping the message of the story for each of us personally is that we already know how it ends: "Lazarus. He's the guy who is raised from the dead. Everyone knows that!" The disciples in the story, however, do not "know that" when they hear that Lazarus has died! They do not know what the outcome will be as they walk with Jesus to the grave in Bethany.

Let's try to look at the story through their eyes and, through our imaginations, live it with them.

## The Message Is Sent

Martha and Mary know Jesus well and are confident in His love for them. They are also aware of His power to heal the sick. So when their brother falls ill, their response is to send word to Jesus—almost certainly with the expectation that He will come quickly and all will be well.

> Now a man named Lazarus was sick. He was from Bethany, the village of Mary and her sister Martha. This Mary, whose brother Lazarus now lay sick, was the same one who poured perfume on the Lord and wiped his feet with her hair. So the sisters sent word to Jesus, "Lord, the one you love is sick."
>
> John 11:1–3

When Jesus receives the news, He makes a proclamation: "This sickness will not end in death. No, it is for God's glory so that God's Son may be glorified through it" (verse 4).

I imagine that the disciples are pleased with this announcement and rejoice once again in the power and love of Jesus.

They can rest assured that all will be well. Jesus is in control; there is no need to be anxious for their friend and his family. They have seen Jesus heal people simply by speaking a word without needing to be in the presence of the sick individual (the centurion's servant, for example). Surely their expectation is to find a healthy Lazarus when they next visit Bethany.

"Jesus loved Martha and her sister and Lazarus. Yet when he heard that Lazarus was sick, he stayed where he was two more days" (verses 5–6). The disciples spend two days with Jesus somewhere outside Judea and away from the Jews in that region.

We have no information about what occurs during these two days, but, undoubtedly, they see the usual things that happen in the presence of Jesus—healings, miracles, freedom, compassion, extraordinary teaching that stretches the mind. Maybe they have time simply to relax together as well. I do not think that Lazarus features much in their thinking at this point; after all, Jesus said that all will be well. They feel no great haste to visit Bethany. In fact, it is safer not to.

## Odd Timing

But then Jesus surprises them.

> He said to his disciples, "Let us go back to Judea."
>
> "But Rabbi," they said, "a short while ago the Jews tried to stone you, and yet you are going back there?"
>
> Jesus answered, "Are there not twelve hours of daylight? A man who walks by day will not stumble, for he sees by this world's light. It is when he walks by night that he stumbles, for he has no light."
>
> John 11:7–10

Imagine the disciples' conversations among themselves: "Judea! Why go back now? There is only trouble waiting for us in Judea. The Jews there are ready to stone Jesus to death. Who knows what might happen to us? We have no urgent reason to go back. Let's see if the Master will agree to stay here for now, where it's safe."

This is an entirely reasonable plan. Thus, they probably scratch their heads at Jesus' response: "Our friend Lazarus has fallen asleep; but I am going there to wake him up" (verse 11).

This does not seem like a great reason to return to Judea. If Lazarus is "sleeping off" his illness, why risk life and limb to pay him a visit? His disciples reply: "Lord, if he sleeps, he will get better" (verse 12). He is on the road to recovery. . . . What's the problem? Why do You need to go and wake him up—surely his sisters can do that at the appropriate time?

Now for the bombshell.

> Jesus had been speaking of his death, but his disciples thought he meant natural sleep. So then he told them plainly, "Lazarus is dead, and for your sake I am glad I was not there, so that you may believe. But let us go to him."
>
> John 11:13–15

Now imagine the disciples' questions.

"Lazarus is dead! How can that be? You told us he wouldn't die. Jesus, did You lie to us? Have You lost Your power and authority over sickness? What do You mean You are glad You were not there? We thought You loved this family!"

This episode could shake their faith to the core. If Jesus knew Lazarus was going to die, why did He not do something? Why did He not go straightaway? What happened to His love and compassion?

Put yourself in the disciples' places. What would you be thinking?

Most of us Christians have experienced times when we believe we have heard something from Jesus and generate expectation in our heads about how God will work it out. Then things turn out differently. How do we respond in those situations?

Let's look at what Jesus actually said when He heard that Lazarus was sick: *This sickness will not end in death.* In other words, "Lazarus is dead, but we are not yet at the end of the story."

It is easy to make judgments halfway through what God is doing. It is much better, I would suggest, to let the story unfold to its conclusion.

Thomas, at this point, makes a suggestion. "Then Thomas (called Didymus) said to the rest of the disciples, 'Let us also go, that we may die with him'" (verse 16).

Have you ever come up with a stupid remark when you are confused? This is a classic example of just that. Thomas thinks through what he is experiencing and somehow decides that it would be a good idea for all the disciples to die, just as Lazarus has died. He reaches a conclusion and volunteers an answer for the whole group. I think this is undoubtedly not a popular conclusion with the rest of the disciples!

The Bible does not give us Jesus' response to this remark. Maybe He says nothing. But He certainly does something.

> On his arrival, Jesus found that Lazarus had already been in the tomb for four days. Bethany was less than two miles from Jerusalem, and many Jews had come to Martha and Mary to comfort them in the loss of their brother.
>
> John 11:17–19

Jesus and His disciples appear to be too late. Lazarus has been in the tomb for four days. Many Jews have arrived to comfort

Martha and Mary, and it is likely that they greet the newcomers and converse with them about the tragedy.

Imagine the disciples trying to answer the inevitable questions:

"How did Jesus respond when He heard the news?"

"What did He say?"

"Why did He wait?"

"What did you do during those two days?"

"'Not end in death' you say!"

It has to be awkward, even embarrassing. The disciples might be tempted to come up with some excuses for Jesus, to protect Him. It is not always easy being with Jesus. Sometimes He is hard to understand.

## The Sisters Respond

Now prepare to meet a remarkable woman.

> When Martha heard that Jesus was coming, she went out to meet him, but Mary stayed at home. "Lord," Martha said to Jesus, "if you had been here, my brother would not have died. But I know that even now God will give you whatever you ask."
>
> John 11:20–22

Martha has great faith. We do not know the tone in which she speaks to Jesus, but from verse 22 we can detect faith and trust. Undoubtedly she expresses sadness, but also brave acceptance of what has happened, lack of bitterness and continuing trust in Jesus. Remarkable.

Martha is completely confident that if Jesus had arrived before her brother died, He would have been able to heal him. And even though Lazarus has died, she knows that God will answer Jesus' prayers, whatever He asks.

But her thinking is limited. It seems that she has not considered that you can ask for the dead to be raised.

Jesus tells her, "Your brother will rise again" (verse 23). He is starting to sow a seed of thought in her mind.

Martha ponders this and says, "I know he will rise again in the resurrection at the last day" (verse 24).

Her response is entirely accurate and reasonable. She is processing what Jesus is saying through what she already knows. Her hope regarding the future is secure. What she says is true, but her knowledge is incomplete. A further level of truth is going to be revealed to her. Jesus is about to bring future hope into present reality.

Jesus tells her, "I am the resurrection and the life. He who believes in me will live, even though he dies; and whoever lives and believes in me will never die. Do you believe this?" (verses 25–26).

Jesus takes hold of a concept, an abstract reality, and personifies it in Himself: *I am the resurrection.* Until this moment, *resurrection* is part of a theology that promises eternal life sometime in the future. Jesus is declaring that in Him is found the reality of eternal life—not in the future but here and now.

Martha responds bravely: "'Yes, Lord,' she told him, 'I believe that you are the Christ, the Son of God, who was to come into the world'" (verse 27).

But she has not quite grasped it.

After she had said this, she went back and called her sister Mary aside. "The Teacher is here," she said, "and is asking for you." When Mary heard this, she got up quickly and went to him. Now Jesus had not yet entered the village, but was still at the place where Martha had met him. When the Jews who had been with Mary in the house, comforting her, noticed how quickly she got up and went out, they followed her, supposing she was going to the tomb to mourn there.

> When Mary reached the place where Jesus was and saw him, she fell at his feet and said, "Lord, if you had been here, my brother would not have died."
>
> John 11:28–32

Jesus asks to see Mary as well, with whom He has a special relationship. On a previous visit, she stayed at Jesus' side, learning from Him while Martha was distracted by preparations in the kitchen (see Luke 10:38–42; we will look at this story in a later chapter). Mary is also the one who will soon anoint Jesus' feet with perfume and dry them with her hair (see John 12:1–3). She appears to be more demonstrative in her relationship with Jesus, falling at His feet as she meets Him here near the tomb. And her response of faith and trust is as strong as her sister's. She, too, affirms that Jesus could have saved her brother from dying.

> When Jesus saw her weeping, and the Jews who had come along with her also weeping, he was deeply moved in spirit and troubled. "Where have you laid him?" he asked.
>
> "Come and see, Lord," they replied.
>
> John 11:33–34

Jesus is moved and troubled by the emotion that He is witnessing. It is not fully clear what this means, but we can conclude that Jesus is touched by other people's feelings and that He has emotions Himself, as we see in the next verse: "Jesus wept" (verse 35).

Imagine what the disciples are thinking now:

"Jesus is crying; why is He crying?"

"This doesn't look good."

"I think we just joined the funeral."

"What now?"

The Jews observe Jesus crying and acknowledge His love for Lazarus, but a good question follows. "Then the Jews said, 'See how he loved him!' But some of them said, 'Could not he who opened the eyes of the blind man have kept this man from dying?'" (verse 36–37). Maybe some are doubting Jesus' love; after all He could have healed Lazarus if He had arrived in time. Not to mention the fact that He did not make the effort to come right away when Martha and Mary asked.

If we are honest, we probably realize that we would have similar questions in their places. Or, being even more honest, we probably have similar questions today, trying to match up the love of God with delays, unanswered requests, confusion. It is difficult sometimes.

> Jesus, once more deeply moved, came to the tomb. It was a cave with a stone laid across the entrance. "Take away the stone," he said.
>
> "But, Lord," said Martha, the sister of the dead man, "by this time there is a bad odor, for he has been there four days."
>
> John 11:38–39

Martha does not understand what Jesus is talking about. Her hope has not yet made its journey from the future to the present. She is concerned with a practical reality: This is going to get smelly!

Imagine the disciples again. What are they thinking now?

Is faith stirring in them that something remarkable is about to happen? Could this be what Jesus was talking about? Is this story not yet finished?

Then Jesus asks a pivotal question: "Did I not tell you that if you believed, you would see the glory of God?" (verse 40). The glory of God is about to become clearly visible.

## The Kingdom Has Come

Once again Jesus is taking an abstract concept and bringing it into visible reality. A reference to the glory of God would bring to the Jewish mind images like mountains on fire, places so holy that no one can enter, unapproachable light.

But how do they qualify to see it? What does it look like? Jesus says that in order to see it all they have to do is believe.

> So they took away the stone. Then Jesus looked up and said, "Father, I thank you that you have heard me. I knew that you always hear me, but I said this for the benefit of the people standing here, that they may believe that you sent me."
>
> John 11:41–42

Jesus wants to lift those around Him to new heights of faith and understanding. Martha, Mary and the disciples have great faith and great hope regarding the future, but Jesus is taking them on a journey of faith so that they will believe something even greater: the Kingdom of heaven being expressed on earth. Death has met its match.

"When he had said this, Jesus called in a loud voice, 'Lazarus, come out!' The dead man came out, his hands and feet wrapped with strips of linen, and a cloth around his face" (verses 43–44). Jesus talks to a dead man, but this story is not going to end in death. He already knows the end of the story, though He has not explained it. He has waited for the right moment in order for the glory of God to be manifested more clearly on the earth.

He raises His voice and gives a command. Life is restored. Jesus uses His authority once again to create life, just as He did during the days of Creation.

38

Imagine the scene.

Tears.

Laughter.

Astonishment.

Realization—Jesus was right all along.

Awe.

They have just seen the glory of God manifested. But what have they actually seen? The love and power of God changing earthly reality and perspectives and opening the realms of eternity. The glory of God here and now.

Jesus has taken people with great faith and made it possible for them to experience more. But the story is not yet complete. Jesus says, "Take off the grave clothes and let him go" (verse 44).

Lazarus is alive, but he is not yet free to live. He cannot see because of the cloth around his face. His hands and feet are bound by strips of linen.

Jesus asks the people around Him to complete Lazarus' freedom. I imagine they participate joyfully, unwrapping Lazarus to enable him to live the life Jesus has given him—privileged to take part in the restoration of life itself.

## Greater Things?

The end of this story gives a picture of the way in which Jesus allows His followers to join in His work. In John 14:12 Jesus states that anyone who has faith in Him will do the works that He has been doing—*and more!* This verse has challenged my thinking enormously over the last few years.

Jesus expects us to do works not only equivalent to His, but also greater. I was taught for many years that this is not possible because it makes us like Jesus, but I have come to realize that such thinking denies biblical truth. Every Christian is called to do the works of Jesus—and, in fact, even greater works than He did during His time living on earth. What an amazing privilege!

One of the works Jesus gave to His early followers was the privilege to *unwrap Lazarus*, to set him free. I believe that same task awaits the Church today. Many Christians, even though they are alive because Jesus has called them, are not free to live their Christian lives to the full because they are bound up by ways of thinking and behavior, some of which have been wrapped around the Church for centuries.

The Bible says, "It is for freedom that Christ has set us free" (Galatians 5:1). This verse used to confuse me, as it seems to be simply repeating itself. But I have come to realize that living in the freedom that God has purposed for us is not the experience of every Christian. God is changing that, however, by revealing truth to His Church—and this truth has the power to set us free.

Just as He did for the men and women standing near the grave of Lazarus centuries ago, so today Jesus is giving those who already have a measure of faith in Him the opportunity to realize and understand more of His glorious nature. The result is that we will grow to love and trust Him even more.

Greater things are being revealed. Greater works are going to be done. In order for that to happen we need to be ready to have our minds renewed, transformed to His ways of thinking. We need to be willing to shed any behavior that restricts us from the fullness of God's purposes for us. We need to throw off these things and allow Him to transform us into His likeness with ever-increasing glory.

It is time to unwrap Lazarus.

## Unwrapping the Bonds

How do you respond when you are confused by God?

How can you trust Jesus when you do not understand what is happening?

Is there a thought or behavior restricting you that needs to be unwrapped so you can see more of the glory of God revealed through your life?

# 3

# UNWRAPPING EXPECTATION

## Revealing the Fullness of Our Identity

What's in a name?

Post-natal visits were one of my joys when I worked full-time as a general practitioner in Swanley in the southeast of England with my own list of patients. Having normally been there when the initial good news of pregnancy was announced to an excited Mum-to-be (sometimes Dad was in attendance, too), through the months of pregnancy, up to the time of birth, I enjoyed accompanying my patients on this adventure.

Then news would arrive of the birth, and before long Mum and baby would happily return home from the hospital, having been checked out to make sure all was well—which it generally was. Community midwives would call on them regularly during the first few days. We worked closely together as part of the primary care team—so I would know instantly if there were any difficulties.

During post-natal visits, I would go to the house to check that all was well with Mother and baby, already knowing with some confidence what I would find. Really, it was more of a social occasion, sharing the joy of the family, having a cup of tea, sometimes meeting the dads for the first time and answering any concerns they might have. I used to look forward to these occasions as they provided a welcome break from some of the pressures of medical work. I normally scheduled them for after my morning consultations and visited on a day when I had a bit more time on my hands.

On one particular day I turned up at the house of a young couple whose baby had been born about a week previously. I remembered the mum coming to see me months earlier, hoping that she was pregnant. I had the joy of confirming that this was so and followed her pregnancy as it progressed without problems. News from the hospital and the midwife was good, and I was ready to share in the joy in due course—hopefully with a cup of tea and a biscuit.

I walked up the path to the front door, swinging my briefcase happily, and rang the doorbell. A man whom I presumed to be the father greeted me warmly and welcomed me into the sitting room. I had not met him previously. He explained that his wife was upstairs with the baby and would be down soon. I offered my congratulations on the new arrival, and he set off for the kitchen to put the kettle on, then went upstairs to let his wife know that I had arrived. This was nice. I sat down feeling content and relaxed. A few minutes later he returned with cups of tea for the two of us and sat down opposite me.

"Now, I have an important question," he said.

"Fire away," I replied.

"What will happen if both my wife and I die?"

I was surprised—very surprised. Surely this was not the moment for such somber thoughts? The baby had only just arrived; everybody seemed to be in good health. I collected my thoughts and he looked at me studiously.

"I'm not sure I know how to answer that at this moment in time," I offered.

A blank look stared back at me.

"But that is why we want to talk with you," he continued.

I tried to think of a good answer, but my mind was not in that gear. I was not sure what was expected of me. For once I was at a loss for words.

At that moment the door to the sitting room opened and in came his wife carrying the newborn baby.

"Hello, Doctor," she said cheerfully.

"Doctor!" The word escaped from her husband's lips in a groan, and he turned a bright shade of red. "I thought you were the life insurance salesman!"

His wife sat down in a chair laughing, her laughter increasing as she heard her husband apologizing profusely for not knowing who I was and for the question he had asked. I laughed as well and the atmosphere lightened and turned to joyful thoughts about the new life that was in the room and all the hopes and dreams that would unfold as time went on.

What the husband expected of me changed the instant he got my identity correct. I was not there to help him think about what to do if a tragedy occurred. I was there to help ensure a healthy life that could be lived to the full.

Recently I was out on the streets of a certain town with a friend looking to share the love and power of God with those we had occasion to meet. We wandered into a cafeteria that was owned by a Christian and chatted with the woman behind the counter. Then we asked her if there was anything she would like us to pray for. She said that she had a medical problem and would appreciate prayer. My friend asked her if she would like to give us some more details, but she declined, not wishing to share her medical history.

I volunteered the information that I was a doctor, and immediately the situation changed. The woman opened up completely about her illness and her struggle with it, engaging me in conversation. My friend stood openmouthed and full of wonder. The title *doctor* has amazing power and trust attached to it. Once this woman believed (correctly, I am glad to say) that I would understand her and possess some ability to help, her expectation of our encounter increased markedly. It is amazing what a title can do.

Whom you believe a person to be and what you believe that he/she can do forms the basis of trusting relationships. That is what faith is fundamentally about—a trusting relationship.

We have relationships with people and with things. When I was a teenager, for instance, my mother had an old, rather unreliable car. We named the car *Will it?* When we wanted to use it for a journey we would ask ourselves the question, Will it or won't it start? Our expectation was one of uncertainty. We were grateful whenever it worked and unsurprised when it did not! Eventually Will it? was traded in for a more reliable model. Strangely we were sad at its departure from our lives; it seemed to take some of the adventure away.

Many people have a relationship with God like this. They are grateful when He works, but not surprised when He does not, according to their frame of reference. Their expectation regarding God is low. I would like to suggest that one of the reasons for this is a case of *mistaken identity*.

Do we really know who God is?

Is He a life insurance policy or a giver of life?

Is Jesus really the same today as He was when He walked on the earth?

Does He still heal the sick and do miracles?

What is our expectation of Him?

All of us exercise faith every day. It is simply a matter of expectation. We exercise faith in our cars, our roads, our banks, our own abilities and the abilities of others. Everyone has faith. The issue is where that faith is placed.

A drug addict will place his faith in a "fix" in order to face life and lift his mood. Patients place their trust in doctors, nurses and other medical professionals for their health needs. Parents trust teachers to educate their children. When our trust appears to be misplaced and we feel let down by someone, then our faith in that person decreases. When trust is rewarded with good service and good outcomes then our faith grows. What I know about a person will determine whether or not a journey of faith can begin and how it will progress.

Mick is our garage mechanic; our expectation of him is very high. We first got to know him about 24 years ago when we moved to the area in the southeast of England where we now live. At that time our two cars had varying reliability and we needed someone we could trust to help us, as I am no mechanic. (That is one area of life where people who know me will definitely avoid asking for my help!)

We soon discovered that Mick is honest, reliable and generous. Not having much clue about cars ourselves, we could easily have been vulnerable to someone unscrupulous.

But we found Mick.

If we phoned him about a problem, he would tell us to bring the car down so he could look at it, then tell us if something needed doing. If he could fix it in a few minutes, he would often do it there and then and sometimes not even charge us. He would tell us if something was serious or if it could wait. If he said, "I wouldn't drive my children around in that," that was good enough for us.

One time we bought a secondhand car and asked Mick to check it over. He told us that it was a good buy and that the gearbox might need changing at some point, but there was no hurry. Every year we used to ask him if the gearbox was okay, and every year he would reply that it did not need replacing yet. He could easily have told us that the work was necessary and we would not have known any different. But he is Mick, and we know he is honest. We never did have to replace that gearbox!

We trust Mick implicitly with our cars; our expectation of his work is high. Just the other day we left one of our cars with him while we went abroad, knowing that he would do what was necessary. I am not looking forward to when he retires. Replacing Mick will be a tall order!

I loved being a medical student. Learning all about the human body was fascinating and being with so many good friends on the journey toward becoming doctors was great fun. It was also fun being with so many other friends studying other subjects, and living in the beautiful city of Bristol was a great joy. So many great memories.

One of the excitements of our first year was the opportunity to visit the local hospital's Accident and Emergency Department one evening for as long into the night as we chose. (The idea of staying up through the night helping with any emergency that might arise had a strange sense of glamour and prestige at that stage—a notion that soon changed when we had to do it on a regular basis.)

We medical students had to pair up in teams and get our names down on a rota, showing who was to do what. I was fortunate to pair up with Susanna, who became one of my best friends at the university. On the evening in question, we set off to Bristol Royal Infirmary with a sense of self-importance and expectation. We reported to the nurse in charge of the department, were greeted warmly and assigned to follow one of the doctors around. This we happily did. We wanted to make our-selves useful; after all we were medical students. But we soon came to realize that we knew virtually nothing helpful.

We looked on and grew in respect for the people working in this environment, who calmly moved from one emergency to another, providing comfort and solutions. The staff were excellent with us and gave us a great experience, which opened our eyes to the world we were entering. They also knew that we were first-year medical students and their low level of expectation was entirely appropriate.

Another friend of ours, on his turn there, asked one of the nurses if he could help. She thought she would give him an easy task, asking him to take a urine sample from a patient. He set off with enthusiasm to find a bottle suitable for collecting a sample, found one and delivered it to the patient, who had to remain in bed while providing the sample because of her medical condition.

This friend of ours returned with the sample, very pleased with himself for helping, at which point the nurses began to laugh uproariously. He had brought back a bottle with a sample in it, but the patient was a woman and the bottle was for a man. (Women's samples are collected a bit differently!) How this woman positioned herself while in bed, to accurately fill the bottle remains a mystery, but it was rightly concluded that no matter what else was wrong with her, her sense of balance was fine. The nurses had a good laugh and the low level of expectation regarding first-year medical students was confirmed once again.

As the years in medical school passed, however, experience and knowledge grew, and the expectations placed upon us grew to some degree as well. We were slowly being prepared to enter the medical workplace—the pressurized environment of hospital medicine. I think, however, that nothing could have prepared us fully for the shock of life after qualification.

I remember a lecture that we received just before our final exams. The lecturer stated that our lives were about to change. At that time we were students and people know what to expect of students, but in a few weeks we would be doctors. Our identity was about to change and with it would come huge expectations. We would no longer be learners; rather we would be givers of life.

It is time to unwrap the bindings of mistaken identity and replace them with the wonder of our identity as children of God. This is the subject of our next three chapters.

## Unwrapping the Bonds

What is your expectation of Jesus regarding miracles in your life?

Has your perception of your own identity ever changed?

How would you describe God's identity?

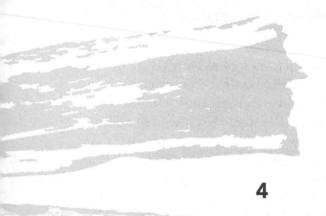

# 4

# UNWRAPPING GOD THE FATHER

## Revealing the Children of God

He forgot who he was.

Let's use our imaginations and other parts of our brains once again as we look at a familiar passage from the Bible to learn more about our true identity. This story in Luke 15 has been named by most Bible commentators the Parable of the Prodigal Son. But does that particular title actually help us understand Jesus' message? It is interesting to note how much influence labels can have on our thinking.

Would you ever feel free to suggest a different title for this parable or would you fear a huge intake of breath from your hearers? Risking a sharp intake of breath from my readers, I would like to suggest this story be renamed the Parable of the Good Dad. Maybe it will catch on.

Let's have a look at the passage and see what we think. Is Jesus' major lesson here drawn from the attitudes and behavior of the younger son? Or perhaps the older son? Or, rather, from the amazing father we meet in the story? Is the central theme "sin" or "generosity"?

Let's do some Bible study.

> Jesus continued: "There was a man who had two sons. The younger one said to his father, 'Father, give me my share of the estate.' So he divided his property between them. Not long after that, the younger son got together all he had, set off for a distant country and there squandered his wealth in wild living."
>
> Luke 15:11–13

Here is a rich man. He owns an estate and has servants. My imagination paints a picture of him as a noble man of good standing in his community.

Of his two sons, the younger one is ready for adventure. He is an immature young man, aware of the riches potentially available to him, but unaware of the responsibility of such privilege. He wants to do things his way, and devises a plan to gain the resources to make that possible. It is a picture that rings true for many young people in generation after generation. Growing into maturity is not always easy, and material wealth does not necessarily make it easier, although poverty has nothing to commend it.

This younger son asks his father to give him his share of the estate, which is considerable.

It is important to note at this point to whom the father gives his estate: Both sons receive equal portions, as the property is divided between them. What will they do with such wealth? We know nothing about the older brother until later in the story, but right away we get a clear picture of the younger brother.

## The Fun Begins

This young man cashes in his wealth, realizes his assets and sets off to have a good time. No longer restricted by any sense of responsibility, he travels to a distant country where he squanders his inheritance in "wild living." Later on in the story we get some clues as to what that looks like. We can use our imaginations as well.

He is probably popular with his newfound friends. And I expect people take advantage of his youth and inexperience—until his money runs out! At that point the picture changes and misery starts to set in: "After he had spent everything, there was a severe famine in that whole country, and he began to be in need" (verse 14).

This is a young man who has likely never known what it is to be in need. His money is gone and, worse still, a severe famine has enveloped the land. His popularity is over. He is hungry. He is a long way from home. No help is at hand. He is on his own.

He starts to search for a solution.

> "So he went and hired himself out to a citizen of that country, who sent him to his fields to feed pigs. He longed to fill his stomach with the pods that the pigs were eating, but no one gave him anything."
>
> Luke 15:15–16

Imagine the sense of shock. Hiring himself out! He grew up surrounded by servants; now he is a laborer. We do not know what sort of work he did in the past, but we can be reasonably certain that at the end of the day, he returned home to a good meal.

Imagine the shame of feeding pigs—those unclean animals a good Jew would avoid. Not only is he feeding them, but their food is somehow appealing. How far can you fall? How desperate can you get? Imagine the despair. Imagine such hunger.

And no one is willing to help him.

No one?

There is no meal and no home—or is there?

His mind starts to wander back to a distant land, and he comes to his senses. Taking a good look around, he says, "How many of my father's hired men have food to spare, and here I am starving to death!" (verse 17).

He thinks back and remembers that even the servants are well fed in his father's household. I can imagine his saliva starting to flow as he remembers the good food, even food to spare. The comparison with his present circumstances must be overwhelming. He is starving to death.

Actually, he does have one thing available to swallow—his pride. This is his only recourse. If he goes back to his father and apologizes, he can seek mercy in accordance with his newfound identity as a servant. After all, he surmises that he is no longer worthy to be called a son. But his dad is a good master, so he can expect to be treated well as a servant and not starve.

> "I will set out and go back to my father and say to him: 'Father, I have sinned against heaven and against you. I am no longer worthy to be called your son; make me like one of your hired men.'"
>
> Luke 15:18–19

Have you ever rehearsed an apology? Going over it again and again in your mind, trying to get it just right, thinking that the perfect words are the most important thing?

Keep rehearsing that speech! Get used to my new identity. . . .

. . . Mistaken identity.

Decision made! Time to get out of this pig field and start walking! "So he got up and went to his father" (verse 20).

I would like to suggest to you that this is the moment of repentance in the story. Coming to his senses, this young man changes his mind and puts repentance into action. Repentance is not demonstrated simply by saying "sorry," but by a change in behavior that results from a change in our thinking.

An apology can be rehearsed, but an action speaks for itself. Every step along the way is a step of redemption.

## The Father's Heart

Now we read the father's reaction to the arrival of his wayward son. "While he was still a long way off, his father saw him and was filled with compassion for him; he ran to his son, threw his arms around him and kissed him" (verse 20).

I sometimes wonder how often this father searches the horizon for sight of his lost son, his eyes straining to discern the shape of every person walking along the road: "Could this be my son?"

Many people pass that way during the time the son is living in that distant land: strangers, friends, people looking for work, even other family members. If they call at the house, it is likely that they receive a warm welcome. Servants will be employed, good times had with friends, but there is a longing in the father's heart that no friend or servant can satisfy.

I think the father looks down that long road every day. How many disappointments does he have to overcome? Straining his eyes as a human form appears in the distance, hope rising. . . . "Perhaps?" Then disappointment once again. Yet he does not allow his hope to die.

Then one day, eyes straining, he sees another person walking along the road, a vague shape coming into view. He watches and the shape becomes a little clearer. His heart rate starts to quicken . . . could it be? Does he recognize that shape? A little thinner maybe, but the way he walks, the swing of his arms. . . .

The father walks toward the figure to get a clearer view; his pace quickens; his mind starts to race; recognition is confirmed.

Can it be true?

Yes!

He breaks into a run. He cannot contain himself. His love, stored up for so long, bursts out of him because the object of his love is within reach. He runs down the road toward his son and throws himself upon him, embracing him, kissing him, laughing, crying.

"My son is home!"

Imagine the son's surprise. This is not the greeting he expects. This is not a greeting fit for a servant! Time for that rehearsed speech. "The son said to him, 'Father, I have sinned against heaven and against you. I am no longer worthy to be called your son'" (verse 21).

Recognition of sin is important, and contrition is an appropriate response, but past sins do not have to dictate our future identity or destiny. This young man rightly understands that he has done wrong, that his thinking and behavior have caused sadness to his father—and also to God. But he is trying to adopt an identity that is not in the heart or mind of his father. He regards himself now as a servant in search of a better master. As many people do, he is allowing his identity to be shaped by his activity rather than his bloodline.

He misunderstands just how full of grace his father is, how willing to forgive and restore. He does not understand that his restoration is in his father's hands, not his own. Hence the rehearsed speech.

"But the father said to his servants, 'Quick! Bring the best robe and put it on him. Put a ring on his finger and sandals on his feet. Bring the fattened calf and kill it. Let's have a feast and celebrate. For this son of mine was dead and is alive again; he was lost and is found.' So they began to celebrate."

Luke 15:22–24

What an amazing dad!

"My son is home. We must celebrate!" His joy is overwhelming and the restoration of his son is immediate. Only the best robe will do.

And what about that ring? Rings given in this way signify covenant love and authority. The son probably sold his previous ring, but his father is only too pleased to restore the covenant relationship and give authority to his son once again. It appears that he takes no notice of that well-rehearsed speech! The relationship has been dead, but now is alive. It is time to party.

## A Greater Waste?

In another of His parables, Jesus makes clear that there is rejoicing in heaven when a sinner repents. In this Parable of the Good Dad, He gives us a picture of such rejoicing. Heaven is a happy place, and so is this restored household. This is going to be a great party. But someone does not want to join in.

"Meanwhile, the older son was in the field. When he came near the house, he heard music and dancing. So he called one of the servants and asked him what was going on. 'Your brother has come,' he replied, 'and your father has killed the fattened calf because he has him back safe and sound.'"

Luke 15:25–27

The older brother comes in from his work. As he approaches the house, the party is in full swing. Music, dancing, probably the aroma of cooked meat reaching his nostrils. What could the occasion be?

He asks one of the servants for an explanation. His brother has come back home, and his father is so happy that he has thrown a party and killed the fattened calf. What? That squanderer has dared to come home—and his father is happy?

At this point he has a choice to make. Will love direct his thoughts and actions—love for his brother, love for his father? Will he rejoice in grace lavished upon his brother by his extravagant father? Or will bitterness and self-pity take over?

Sadly, the latter is the case. Anger is the overriding emotion for this man. He refuses to join the party.

Why should he rejoice?

What about fairness and justice?

Over the years I have spoken with many Christians about this story. It is not uncommon to hear a good deal of sympathy for the older brother. "I can understand how he must have felt" is a common response.

Less commonly expressed is disapproval of the father's attitude and actions, but, nonetheless, this is implied by agreeing with the brother's sentiments.

Grace is offensive to a mind set on justice.

*It's not fair!* is a cry that might ring out.

No, it is not fair—and am I grateful!

My relationship with God is based on His amazing, fabulous, extravagant grace, lavished upon me, that not only forgives my sin but restores me to a place of sonship, with rejoicing, provision and authority to carry out the family business of heaven, my eternal home.

That makes me happy!

Unfortunately, it does not make the older brother happy, so this great dad reaches out to him, because he wants this son to share in the rejoicing. In fact, his father goes out and pleads with him to come in.

Once again this older son has the opportunity to enter into his father's happiness, to be drawn into this realm of grace. His response is extremely sad. In actual fact, it is not one worthy of a son!

> "He answered his father, 'Look! All these years I've been slaving for you and never disobeyed your orders. Yet you never gave me even a young goat so I could celebrate with my friends. But when this son of yours who has squandered your property with prostitutes comes home, you kill the fattened calf for him!'"
>
> Luke 15:29–30

In his mind he has been "slaving" for his father. What sort of relationship is this?

This son has identified himself as a slave (not even a servant) who must obey orders from a demanding master. These are not the words of a son who knows his identity and the grace and generosity of his father. He does not even expect that his father would give him a goat to eat with his friends (and trust me, goat meat does not bear any comparison to beef!).

He has a completely wrong view of his father. But more than that, he does not realize that he already has more than he needs. Remember that his father has divided his property between his sons. This older brother has had access to exactly the same resources as his younger brother from the beginning of the story, yet he does not avail himself of it. He squanders his inheritance in a different way—through lack of use. He

UNWRAPPING GOD THE FATHER

has wasted the amazing opportunity of an inheritance that is already available to him.

The Bible teaches us clearly that Christians are children of God. In addition to that, we are heirs. The Christian message contains more than just forgiveness of sins; it also contains sonship—intimate relationship with God and an inheritance that is already given to us.

I am currently pursuing the discovery of the full extent of my inheritance from God, because for so many years as a Christian I did not realize the enormity of it. Nowadays, I boldly approach the throne of God—not on an occasional basis for forgiveness and mercy, but on a regular basis to place my requests and claim my inheritance. Miracles are becoming part of the normal Christian life: eyesight restored, deafness gone, a mute boy speaking, a man who was brain-dead now alive, knees healed, asthma gone, a leg ulcer healing in a miraculously short space of time—these are some of the things we have seen and heard in our circle of friends within three months of writing these words.

How do you respond to such things?

What if I tell you that some of these things happened through the prayers of people who have just returned to God, having wandered away for some time?

Do you think: "That's not fair! I have been praying for years and have never seen anyone healed!"

Traces of the older brother can creep into any one of us, thinking that our faithful service to God—all that work and all those prayers—somehow means that we deserve to see miracles.

God's goodness and provision is released into our lives through His grace, not through our works. He loves us as His children, and He wants us to use our inheritance to enrich the lives of those around us by making the resources of heaven available.

Listen to words of this father: "'My son,' the father said, 'you are always with me, and everything I have is yours'" (verse 31).

What a statement! Then these astonishing words: "'But we had to celebrate and be glad, because this brother of yours was dead and is alive again; he was lost and is found'" (verse 32).

## The Resources Are Available!

At this time in world history, God is revealing much to His people. The revelation of His Father heart toward us and the revelation of the Kingdom of heaven being expressed on earth are, to my mind, changing the shape and experience of Christianity. They are two key aspects of the new wineskin that is needed to contain the new wine of His Spirit being poured out on the world. They are two of the strands vital to unwrapping the unhelpful thinking that keeps Lazarus bound.

Let us take off the bindings of the slave mentality, which perceives that God is searching for servants rather than sons.

Let us also take off the bindings of believing that we have to work to gain our inheritance. Instead, let us understand that the resources of the Kingdom of heaven are at our disposal—and that our Father in heaven is more than happy for us to use them.

These resources are available because of the life, death, resurrection and ascension of Jesus. He has paid the price, and His grace has set us free. It is time to heal the sick, set people free, raise the dead and enjoy the goodness and greatness of our Father.

It is time to join the party—it is in full swing in heaven! Do you hear the words of your Father? "We have to celebrate and be glad, because this child of Mine was dead and is alive again; he was lost and is found!"

Let's celebrate the grace of God.

He has found us, made us alive, and we are His forevermore.

Happy, happy, happy.

## Unwrapping the Bonds

Do you see this parable as a lesson about "man's sin" or "God's generosity"?

Have you ever squandered one of God's gifts to you?

Do you see yourself as God's slave or His child?

Can you receive His love?

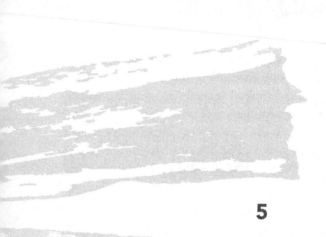

# 5

# UNWRAPPING FAMILY

## *Revealing Family Resources*

His name is David; her name is Kerry.

What is so special about these two people? They have a place in the hearts of my wife, Kim, and me like no other. They are our children.

Kim has the first place in my heart (after God, of course), and we share everything that we have. It does not occur to us to think otherwise; we are one. And our greatest delight together has been to raise our children. David's wife, Jo, now shares in that same affection. And then there are Zoe and Samuel, our grandchildren, and they have a pull on our hearts in the same way. No one can stir us like they can.

Family is an amazing thing, a wonderful thing, something created in heaven, a reflection of the Godhead.

A couple of years ago, a friend from France came to visit us and we welcomed him into our home. With great deliberation he strode into the kitchen and looked at our refrigerator. "This is the famous Carter fridge," he declared.

I smiled, remembering how many times I had referred to our fridge in sermons I had given in France.

Let me explain.

David and Kerry are now adults and have not lived in our family home for a good number of years. They both had "gap years" before college, then college itself, then work in other parts of the country. They would come home at various times, still having their own keys to our house. Sometimes they would visit when we were not there. Our house is their home—it is where they grew up, and they have freedom there that no one else shares.

They feel completely at liberty to raid the fridge. In fact, if we know they are coming home we will stock up the fridge and freezer with things especially for them (and in Kerry's case the fruit bowl as well). We would be disappointed if they did not take advantage of what is available to them.

## Different Expectations

Our children have access to things from us that no one else has—not just material things, but also intimacy, support, fun and emotional resources.

Kim and I love to entertain, and when guests come to stay we ask them to make themselves at home—to feel free to make a drink, use the fridge, help themselves. We genuinely mean it and are delighted to find our friends putting the kettle on, having some cereal, making a sandwich, sitting in the garden. But no matter what we say, they are not going to feel as free and at home as David and Kerry.

If I were a guest I would act much the same way. It would seem perfectly acceptable to get some milk for my coffee, maybe some ice for a drink. But to open that pack of cheese or that bottle of wine . . . ? Normal social etiquette places some appropriate restraint upon us, because it is not our house. But it is different when we are home.

A sense of "home" is one of the reasons why it is so important to know our identity as sons and daughters of God—rather than merely His friends or even servants. It will give us the confidence to access the resources of heaven, our inheritance.

Another reason is with regard to hearing God. Servants hear from their masters, but they expect words of instruction or orders. They do not anticipate words of intimacy.

Sons and daughters expect something different—affirmation, affection, fun, laughter, dreams, plans for holidays, plans for the future, conversation. Plus, a son or daughter will expect not only to hear, but also to be heard.

Most often my conversation with my son or daughter will end with the words *Love you loads* coming from both of us. It is true and it does our hearts good.

## Is God Your Master or Father?

I believe many Christians miss a lot of what God is saying to them because they are expecting instructions prior to any feelings of intimacy. Then they get busy obeying the instructions and miss the closeness. Now, please do not get me wrong: God does give us instructions. But if that is all we hear, we are probably relating to God as a master and not as a Father. Jesus did not instruct us to pray that way!

The story of Martha and Mary is illustrative of this point. We have already met them in the Bible—in the raising of their brother, Lazarus. Let's look at another, earlier, story that involves them.

> As Jesus and his disciples were on their way, he came to a village where a woman named Martha opened her home to him. She had a sister called Mary, who sat at the Lord's feet listening to what he said. But Martha was distracted by all the preparations that had to be made. She came to him and asked, "Lord, don't you care that my sister has left me to do the work by myself? Tell her to help me!"
>
> "Martha, Martha," the Lord answered, "you are worried and upset about many things, but only one thing is needed. Mary has chosen what is better, and it will not be taken away from her."
>
> Luke 10:38–42

Martha is in "servant mode." Consider her situation: Important things need to be done. After all, Jesus is the guest! Imagine the scene in the kitchen—pots boiling away, bread being made, the pressure mounting to get the meal ready. And what about the table? It needs to be set. How about pouring beverages for the thirsty disciples? Where is Mary? Why isn't she helping?

The Bible says that Martha is distracted. Distracted from what? Well, the main event—Jesus is here! She is so busy preparing things for Jesus that she does not have time to be with Jesus. She even gets frustrated with Him: "Don't You care? I am doing all this work for You by myself."

What is Jesus' assessment?

Martha is bound up in worry and frustration because she has forgotten the most important thing: being with Jesus. Please note, Jesus does not say that she has done something wrong, but rather that Mary has chosen something better—to sit at His feet. The meal will get eaten and be gone, but the value of spending time sitting with Jesus will endure.

When our children come home we want to spend time with them, not set them to work in the kitchen or garden.

Kim and I have a housecleaner come to help us about once every two weeks. She is brilliant and does an excellent job. Sometimes I am working at home on those days, and say hello to her. But then she gets on with her work, and I get on with mine. She will get herself something to drink, but she would never consider raiding the fridge. But when my children come home, I stop what I am doing to be with them. We chat. They open the fridge and help themselves. It is a different relationship.

*Are you God's child?*

I like to think of myself as a child of God with a servant heart. That seems to me to be the example that Jesus set for us. As we learned in the last chapter, we have access to the resources of heaven—but this is not simply for our benefit. We can use them for the benefit of others.

If, however, I am missing those resources because I am bound by worry and frustration, then I will not enjoy my spiritual inheritance. If my primary identity is that of a servant waiting on God, having to fend for myself, I will relate to God primarily as a master, missing out on intimacy and many other things.

It is time to unwrap the strips of our servant identity, allow the Holy Spirit within us to cry out "Abba Father," and raid the fridge of heaven—not only to feed our own needs, but also the needs of a hungry world.


## Unwrapping the Bonds

Do you feel close to God? As close as a beloved child should feel?

Are you using the resources He has provided for you?

If you still have a servant identity, how do you unwrap it?

# 6

# UNWRAPPING PRIORITIES

*Revealing the Potential
of the Kingdom of God*

Seek first the Kingdom.

It was January 2009. I had been leading North Kent Community Church in southeast England for more than twenty years, so when someone told me I was fulfilling only 30 percent of my capacity, it came as a bit of a shock.

That person was Kris Vallotton, and the context was a training course for church leadership teams hosted by Bethel Church in Redding, California. Kris, who is senior associate pastor and an overseer of Bethel's School of Supernatural Ministry, came into the room, where about fifty of us were sitting. In his inimitable way, he told us that God had just shown him we were all working at only 30 percent of our true potential. All of us!

This room was filled with "successful church leaders"! How could this be true?

Quite a bold statement from Kris, you might think, and, indeed, I did think that. But something deep inside me knew that it was true. I was strangely stirred. What was the Holy Spirit saying to me?

This all came as a surprise because I regarded myself as a hardworking and relatively successful individual. North Kent Community Church had helped the Body of Christ in many ways over the years—including helping many other churches in their births, development and progress. We were a relatively large congregation and had some good projects running.

All these thoughts ran through my mind in the few seconds before Kris explained that we were all missing our potential. "The reason for this," Kris continued, "is that you are doing the wrong job!"

*Whoa, there! God called me to do this!* I thought (along with about 49 other people in my estimation). *I gave up my partnership in a medical practice to do this.* Various other thoughts flashed through my mind. Now I felt confused.

Again, just a few seconds passed before Kris explained further: "That is because you think it is your job to build the Church."

*That's right! That is my job,* I thought, feeling a little safer. This was more comfortable, but I had a suspicion that my comfort was about to be disrupted.

Kris was ready for the finale: "Jesus said that He would build the Church. Our job is to seek first the Kingdom of God and extend it to others."

*Oh, no,* I thought. *That changes everything.*

My mind was now racing, but deep inside I was convinced that God had just spoken something profound to me—something that would shake the foundations of my life and my work.

Did Jesus really say, "*I will build My Church*"?
He certainly did.

> "And I tell you that you are Peter, and on this rock I will build
> my church, and the gates of Hades will not overcome it. I will
> give you the keys of the kingdom of heaven; whatever you bind
> on earth will be bound in heaven, and whatever you loose on
> earth will be loosed in heaven."
>
> Matthew 16:18–19

Jesus is going to build His Church. Our part has to do with
the keys of the Kingdom of heaven. Jesus certainly uses us in
this process, so this was not an argument for non-involvement
in church (which would be counterproductive). Rather, for me
this was a wake-up call in terms of priorities and greater faith
in Jesus.

Some months previously I had found it quite amusing when
a friend, a church leader in England, heard God tell him, *I want
My job back*. My friend was stirred by this. Now it was my turn.

## The Right Mindset

In Matthew 6:33 Jesus instructs us to seek first the Kingdom,
alternately worded the Kingdom of God and the Kingdom of
heaven. The question in my mind was, *Am I seeking first the
Kingdom, or am I seeking first to build North Kent Community
Church and other churches connected to us?*

Did I have a "Kingdom-first mindset" or a "Church-first
mindset"?

Please hear me right: This is not about the abandonment of
church. Rather my mind was being expanded.

As you have already read in this book, I love my children and
they know that. They also know, however, that the love that

Kim and I have for each other exceeds even that which we have for them. This was and is important for them. Our philosophy is that our healthy marriage is the bedrock for our safe family environment. Our children appreciate this and know it does not diminish them in any way. Rather, it gave them a healthy environment to grow up in. We want them to carry forward that philosophy into their marriages and family life.

In a similar sense, to prioritize the Kingdom above the Church does not reduce the Church in any way. Rather, it sets the Church in a healthy environment within which it can grow and develop.

Later that day I talked with the fellow leaders of our church who were also in that training course. We started to discuss the challenge that had just been placed in front of us. So began a journey for North Kent Community Church.

It is a journey that has challenged us in almost every area of life. It has challenged us over the message that we are trying to convey. It has driven us back to study the Bible in greater depth. It has brought us into great freedom and delight. But we have had to be willing to pay the price of change.

Another good friend of mine, Dave King, puts it this way: He likens church life to living in a zoo! In a zoo (at least in a good one) animals are well fed, secure, given excellent veterinary care, put on show and even given the opportunity to reproduce. What more could they want? But is this what they were created for? And if they do reproduce, what sort of life will their offspring inherit?

Somehow, over the course of time, the concept of church has shifted from being a training ground where people can learn to draw on the resources of the Kingdom of heaven, enabling them to live in the freedom God has given to them, to being a safe environment, producing well-fed Christians, helping them with their problems and even giving them the chance to reproduce through evangelistic opportunities.

In more recent times, zoos have become a little less acceptable and a new kind of animal sanctuary has arisen—the safari park! This looks different, but is fundamentally the same, just with more space for the animals to express themselves and a more interactive experience for the visitors. The animals, however, were still not created to live in such confines. They were made for free living in their native habitats, facing the realities of a sometimes difficult existence.

*Freedom is a big thing!*

Adopting a Kingdom-first mindset redresses this issue by putting Christianity in its right context.

More recently, I was playing squash with a friend. As we were having our after-match drink, I told him that I was writing a book (this book!). He was intrigued and asked me what it was about. This led to a discussion during which he told me that his wife hates going to church because it makes her angry. He went on to explain that she really objects to "being made to feel guilty" and "told that she is a rotten sinner."

I had to agree with him—that does not sound like Good News. Unfortunately, this is not an uncommon experience. People expect Christians to make them feel bad about themselves.

What message is the Church preaching?

Is it the same message that Jesus preached and that He instructed His disciples to preach?

Has our preoccupation become people's sin rather than Jesus and the Kingdom of heaven?

Are we trying to do the work of the Holy Spirit, instead of trusting Him to do it? Jesus said clearly that the Holy Spirit will convict people of sin. Maybe He wants His job back as well?

The New Testament message, particularly evident in the gospels, is a message of the Kingdom of God. Also, throughout the book of Acts we see an emphasis on the message of the Kingdom of God.

After [Jesus'] suffering, he showed himself to these men and gave many convincing proofs that he was alive. He appeared to them over a period of forty days and spoke about the kingdom of God.

Acts 1:3

But when they believed Philip as he preached the good news of the kingdom of God and the name of Jesus Christ, they were baptized, both men and women.

Acts 8:12

Paul entered the synagogue and spoke boldly there for three months, arguing persuasively about the kingdom of God.

Acts 19:8

[Paul said,] "Now I know that none of you among whom I have gone about preaching the kingdom will ever see me again."

Acts 20:25

They arranged to meet Paul on a certain day, and came in even larger numbers to the place where he was staying. From morning till evening he explained and declared to them the kingdom of God and tried to convince them about Jesus from the Law of Moses and from the Prophets.

Acts 28:23

Boldly and without hindrance [Paul] preached the kingdom of God and taught about the Lord Jesus Christ.

Acts 28:31

So what is this Kingdom? I think the fact that it is described as the "Kingdom of God" and the "Kingdom of heaven" interchangeably throughout Scripture gives us direction in our thinking.

## Where Is Heaven?

Most of us imagine heaven as a place of joy, peace, wonder, beauty and many other desirable things. But what if God were not there—would it still be heaven?

I don't think so.

My house is my home because Kim and I live there. If we were to sell it and someone else moved in, it would no longer be our home. We would establish a new home elsewhere.

Thus, heaven, to me, is not a question of geography. It is defined primarily by God's presence and activity. Wherever He is becomes heavenly. That is why Jesus could say, "Repent, for the kingdom of heaven is near" (Matthew 4:17). When Jesus was near, heaven was near, and the activity of heaven happened. What did this mean practically?

Well, in heaven there is no sickness, so around Jesus sickness disappeared.

In heaven sin cannot exist, so Jesus could proclaim the forgiveness of sins.

Demons are banished from heaven, so Jesus could resist them and banish them from His presence.

This is well illustrated in the story at the beginning of Mark 2:

A few days later, when Jesus again entered Capernaum, the people heard that he had come home. So many gathered that there was no room left, not even outside the door, and he preached the word to them. Some men came, bringing to him a paralytic, carried by four of them. Since they could not get him to Jesus because of the crowd, they made an opening in the roof above Jesus and, after digging through it, lowered the mat the paralyzed man was lying on. When Jesus saw their faith, he said to the paralytic, "Son, your sins are forgiven."

73

Now some teachers of the law were sitting there, thinking to themselves, "Why does this fellow talk like that? He's blaspheming! Who can forgive sins but God alone?"

Immediately Jesus knew in his spirit that this was what they were thinking in their hearts, and he said to them, "Why are you thinking these things? Which is easier: to say to the paralytic, 'Your sins are forgiven,' or to say, 'Get up, take your mat and walk'? But that you may know that the Son of Man has authority on earth to forgive sins. . . ." He said to the paralytic, "I tell you, get up, take your mat and go home." He got up, took his mat and walked out in full view of them all. This amazed everyone and they praised God, saying, "We have never seen anything like this!"

Mark 2:1–12

Jesus demonstrated His authority to forgive sins by healing the paralytic. Both of these activities were derived from heaven and performed with heaven's authority. The teachers of the Law knew correctly that only God could authorize such things. The activity of the Kingdom of heaven caused people to confront the reality of God among them. And that is how it is still meant to be.

Jesus demonstrated the Kingdom of heaven to all around Him. Some liked it; others did not. Remember the woman caught in adultery? The Law demanded her death, but Jesus used heavenly wisdom (more about this later) to overcome death and bring life and hope through mercy and forgiveness.

What does Jesus' presence mean for us today? Jesus is just as interested in our experiencing heaven now as He was for His earthly followers two thousand years ago. He came to unbind us from anything that would inhibit Kingdom living. Galatians 5:1 states that "it is for freedom that Christ has set us free."

Further, Jesus said that the Kingdom is within. Paul emphasized this when he wrote that "the kingdom of God is not a matter of eating and drinking, but of righteousness, peace and joy in the Holy Spirit" (Romans 14:17). The context is whether or not Christians should eat or drink certain things because they might be "unclean." In making his case for not offending one's brother, he distinguishes between external behavior and internal reality. The Kingdom of God affects our internal being, which is then expressed through our attitudes and actions.

Let's look at the three elements that Paul suggested constitute this reality.

### Righteousness

What does it mean to be righteous? One definition is based on 1 John 1:9: "If we confess our sins, he is faithful and just and will forgive us our sins and purify us from all unrighteousness."

When I accepted Jesus, I confessed my sins and asked for God's forgiveness. He not only forgave me but also purified me from all unrighteousness.

What is purity? To my mind, something that is pure is free from contamination. I am no longer contaminated by unrighteousness and sin, which produce guilt, shame and fear. I am free to live my life without my mind being polluted by these things. Instead my mind can be renewed and filled with the thoughts of heaven itself, described in Galatians as the fruit of the Spirit—love, joy, peace, patience, kindness, goodness, faithfulness, gentleness and self-control. Now that is the way to live.

I wake up in the morning knowing that I am free to live this life. That freedom includes choice, of course, and I still make some wrong choices and wander into the pathways of sin. But once I confess this to God, He forgives me and purifies me once again.

The message of the Kingdom is not guilt and shame, but purity; not fearful purity, trying to avoid contamination, but joyful purity bringing life wherever we go. Remember, Jesus' purity was not contaminated by interaction with lepers, but rather made them whole. His purity was not threatened by people's sin. Instead He took away their sin. We can have the same attitude.

### Peace

What is peace? There are many ways to describe it. One of the ways that Jesus expressed it was this: If people would come to Him, He would give them "rest for their souls." This is talking about an inner reality that can sustain us in the middle of any circumstance.

Peace can be described as an absence of conflict. To know such peace inside yourself is a wonderful way to live. It includes freedom from anxiety and preoccupation with human circumstances. Jesus offers us peace that surpasses understanding.

I remember when I first started my university studies. The adjustments in life were enormous. New things to explore, finances to manage, friends to make, a vast amount of knowledge to be acquired, even laundry to do (or not!). Since my mind was preoccupied with such things, my sleeping and waking thoughts were filled with my to-do list. Quite understandable, we might say, but the lack of peace was evident in my life. One night I decided that I needed God's help—not with my to-do list, but with my internal reality. I asked God to wake me up the next morning with His praise on my lips.

And that is what happened. I woke up literally singing a praise song. Peace and joy flooded my being. All of a sudden life was better. The Kingdom of heaven was expressed in me. Freedom flooded my being and my approach to daily life changed. This has remained true to this day.

### Joy

Joy is great stuff! If you look at what the Bible has to say about heaven, it looks like a joyful place. Jesus was anointed with the oil of gladness above His companions—He was happy!

Freedom from misery is a great thing, and it is what is offered in the Kingdom of heaven. How strange it is, then, that church life is associated so frequently with joyless observation of rules and regulations that restrict one's freedom!

I like being joyful and, to be honest, my not being miserable makes life much more pleasant for those around me.

When I first qualified as a doctor and was employed in a hospital, I had to work crazy hours. If I was scheduled over a weekend, I was in the hospital for eighty hours nonstop and was available all that time for emergency and routine work. Sleep was a luxury that you took when it was available, amounting usually to two or three hours per night, interspersed with emergency calls.

I learned to live tired. For me, the worst time was when I was summoned from sleep at about three a.m. That is a dreadful time to be awakened and expected to function well enough to save someone's life! I well remember waking to the sound of the rudely clanging phone, groggily taking the call, wearily rising from my bed, making sure that I was in a decent state to appear before other people and trudging off to the hospital ward to see the patient.

When I awoke I was not happy, but God has given me an amazing resource from heaven, and I put it to good effect. It is called speaking in tongues and it is a way of communicating with God and drawing on His resources without the restriction of human understanding.

I can pray in tongues anytime I choose, and I often do so.

In those early hours of the morning I had a choice to make: Be justifiably grumpy, projecting my tiredness and misery upon others, and create a difficult atmosphere around me, or call on the resources of heaven.

So as I awoke I would start to speak in tongues, and I would continue as I went on my way. People who came across me in the hospital corridors must have wondered what I was muttering about, but it was a happy muttering, for as I allowed the Holy Spirit to work within me I became filled with joy and peace that surpassed human understanding. I could then deal with not only the patients but also the nurses and other staff in a manner that projected peace and calm into the environment. The Kingdom of heaven was near. My reputation became that of the "happy doctor." I like to think that the patients received better treatment and my colleagues had a better working environment because I brought the benefits of the Kingdom with me.

In Paul's letter to the Romans he wrote that this righteousness, joy and peace are "in the Holy Spirit." We shall turn to that issue, one of intimacy, next.

But back to January 2009. What had been natural to me as I worked in a medical environment, extending the benefits of the Kingdom of heaven, was less natural as I worked in the church environment. Had I helped to create a zoo or even a safari park? How could I help to produce a truly *free* environment where people could fulfill all of their God-given potential and live lives that demonstrated the goodness and greatness of God to the world?

I came to realize that my priorities had been wrong. I had a Church-first mindset rather than a Kingdom-first mindset. When I learned to unwrap that misplaced mindset with the help of the Holy Spirit, I could get out of Jesus' way as He built His Church. The added benefit, along with freedom, was intimacy.

## Unwrapping the Bonds

Does "church work" define your experience of Kingdom living?

Do you believe that the Kingdom of heaven is within you? How is God's presence and activity expressed through you?

On a scale of one to ten, where do righteousness, peace and joy rank in your life?

# 7

# UNWRAPPING THE HOLY SPIRIT

*Revealing Intimacy with God*

His name is "Holy Spirit."

One of the joys for me of being a family doctor was getting to know people over a period of time and becoming someone who was trusted and allowed to help them through some of life's issues. I particularly enjoyed getting to know families and seeing them grow.

Sometimes, during the course of my work, it was necessary to visit my patients at home. On a number of occasions I was greeted at the door by someone I had never met, but who knew that I was coming. The person was usually there to help out while someone in the family was ill.

"It's the doctor!" he or she would call out to the patient, who was as yet unseen. I would then be ushered into the relevant room to see the ill person.

The next greeting was usually different from the first: "Hello, Doctor, thank you for coming."

There is a huge difference between "It's the doctor" and "Hello, Doctor." The first is a functional reality, the second a statement of relationship and trust—intimacy. I knew which I preferred.

A few years ago, however, even though I was sensitive to this distinction, my Christian ears began to pick up what I considered to be a strange phrase. I came across people who, when teaching Christian principles and practice, referred to one member of the Godhead simply as *Holy Spirit*. Phrases such as "Holy Spirit will speak to you . . . Holy Spirit will show you . . . Holy Spirit will give you . . ." came from their lips.

*Hold on a minute,* I thought, *He is "the Holy Spirit" if you don't mind!* My sensitivities were being challenged and my comfort disturbed. I had taught a lot about Him during my Christian life, and I had always referred to Him as "the Holy Spirit." That was His correct title, in my opinion. After all, He is God.

As I listened on, though, I realized that these people had an intimate relationship with this Person. He was not a functional reality to them, but God Himself at home with them.

There is a big difference between "It's the Holy Spirit" and "Hello, Holy Spirit."

Another challenge had entered my life: What was my relationship with God really like?

## Understanding This Relationship

The Holy Spirit is the third Person of the Trinity. The doctrine of the Trinity—God is three in one, one in three, eternally one—is a bedrock of Christian belief. We are right to guard this doctrine fiercely. Yet within this concept it seems that Christians tend to settle on a lesser view of the Holy Spirit than of Jesus or the Father. As my friend Julian Adams has put it, sometimes we view the Holy Spirit as "the butler of heaven" rather than God Himself.

If I could actually walk with Jesus for a day on this earth, my expectation would probably be higher than it is with the reality of walking with the Holy Spirit every day. This should not be.

The New Testament is as full of accounts about the Holy Spirit as it is of Jesus and the Father. In fact, Jesus said to His disciples that it was better for them that He go away because He would send the Holy Spirit to them: "But I tell you the truth: It is for your good that I am going away. Unless I go away, the Counselor will not come to you; but if I go, I will send him to you" (John 16:7).

Imagine that! Imagine yourself as one of the disciples who has given up everything to follow Jesus. Now He is going to leave, and says that is a good thing.

What is good about it?

The Counselor will come.

The passage goes on to explain this further:

"When he comes, he will convict the world of guilt in regard to sin and righteousness and judgment: in regard to sin, because men do not believe in me; in regard to righteousness, because I am going to the Father, where you can see me no longer; and in regard to judgment, because the prince of this world now stands condemned.

"I have much more to say to you, more than you can now bear. But when he, the Spirit of truth, comes, he will guide you into all truth. He will not speak on his own; he will speak only what he hears, and he will tell you what is yet to come. He will bring glory to me by taking from what is mine and making it known to you. All that belongs to the Father is mine. That is why I said the Spirit will take from what is mine and make it known to you.

"In a little while you will see me no more, and then after a little while you will see me."

John 16:8–16

Jesus wanted to teach His disciples more, but they were not ready to bear it. Instead, the Spirit of truth would guide them into all truth. The Spirit would take truth from Jesus and reveal it to His disciples.

If that was true for these men who were in close personal contact with Jesus on earth for three years, it is equally true for you and me. Holy Spirit is not a meager substitute for Jesus, sent to take His place on earth because the first choice has left the field of play.

At the beginning of Jesus' public ministry on earth, John the Baptist announced something significant: "After me will come one who is more powerful than I, whose sandals I am not fit to carry. He will baptize you with the Holy Spirit and with fire" (Matthew 3:11).

John summarized Jesus' ministry in this way: He will baptize you with the Holy Spirit and with fire. Jesus' life, death and resurrection made a way for us to receive something special—not just the forgiveness of our sins, but the immersion of our lives into God Himself.

The Holy Spirit is not an impersonal force sent to help us live our Christian lives. He is God living inside us, come to make His home in us. He has been sent to bring us life in all its fullness. All that Jesus made available to us through His life, death, resurrection and ascension, the Holy Spirit can now make real in our lives.

As I said previously, the Kingdom of heaven is manifest wherever God is present. Since the Holy Spirit is present inside me as a Christian, the Kingdom is within me.

## What Difference Does This Make?

If this is true, how then should I live?

A number of years ago I was asked to work with churches in the U.K., France and one or two other places in Europe. I was expected to provide them with input, support and resources in order to help them develop and grow. I had been appointed to a prominent position, and I felt a sense of privilege (and importance!).

I was determined to be faithful with this responsibility and discharge it to the best of my ability (please note the part about "my ability") while remaining faithful to my responsibilities within my own church family.

I worked hard—and I was performing God's work. Whenever people asked me how I was doing, I would proudly announce that I was very busy and recount some details of my recent travels and accomplishments. Somehow, I had come to believe that a hectic lifestyle was important for a church leader, a sort of badge of honor. What church leader would ever say that life was calm and peaceful, relaxed but fruitful, with plenty of time to spend with God and the important people in one's life? Such a stance would immediately raise suspicion! What are you doing with your time?

During those days, I suspect that if you had given me a choice between a church full of "Mary types" or "Martha types" I would definitely have chosen the Marthas. There was work to do!

About six months into this punishing schedule, I began to feel strange inside. I was engaged in all this work for God—and I was fulfilled in one sense—but I was empty in another sense. When did I have time for God Himself?

I remember the day well. It was a Saturday and I was at home. After breakfast, I decided it was time to have a cup of coffee with God and my Bible. I sat down on our couch and started to talk with God, happily sipping on my coffee. I planned to read my Bible and asked God to fill me once again with His presence, love, peace and joy.

I sensed Him say to me, *Why don't you read Galatians?*

*Great idea,* I thought. Not wanting to read just a few verses but rather get the sweep of the whole book, I dug in and enjoyed the truth flowing from the pages under the guidance of Holy Spirit.

- Grace and peace coming from God
- The amazing Good News entrusted to us
- Paul's vigorous defense of the Gospel in chapter 2

Then I got to chapter 3:

> You foolish Galatians! Who has bewitched you? Before your very eyes Jesus Christ was clearly portrayed as crucified. I would like to learn just one thing from you: Did you receive the Spirit by observing the law, or by believing what you heard? Are you so foolish? After beginning with the Spirit, are you now trying to attain your goal by human effort? Have you suffered so much for nothing—if it really was for nothing? Does God give you his Spirit and work miracles among you because you observe the law, or because you believe what you heard?
>
> Galatians 3:1–5

That is strong language. Those foolish Galatians! Imagine making those sorts of mistakes!

I glanced over the words again and as I read verse 3, I heard God's gentle voice: *Are you so foolish?*

And then I realized that this verse was talking directly to me. I had fallen into the trap of trying to attain my goal through my own effort, rather than by the Spirit. I was being foolish. I was so busy working for God that I had forgotten to work with Him.

What example was I placing before others?

What was I doing to myself?

I had taught many times about being filled with the Holy Spirit, but here I was running on empty.

Immediately, I apologized to God and repented, changing my attitude and mindset. I asked to be filled, not as a necessary spiritual energy boost so that I could carry on as before, but rather so that I could be close to Him, know His touch and live my life as per the Maker's instructions.

And then verse 5 struck me. It talks not just about receiving the Spirit, but also about miracles being worked among us. The normal Christian life is one filled with the Spirit and experiencing miracles. All of this is based on the grace of God, lavished upon us.

There is no way that I can produce miracles through my own effort; a life lived in communion with Holy Spirit, however, will naturally include miracles.

This sounded like a better way of life and work.

Miracles are a confirmation of the Good News of Jesus Christ: "So Paul and Barnabas spent considerable time there, speaking boldly for the Lord, who confirmed the message of his grace by enabling them to do miraculous signs and wonders" (Acts 14:3).

I had been busy with my own efforts, and in many ways, I probably looked like a successful leader. But without the supernatural activity of the Holy Spirit in my life, I could not convey the true message of Christianity in its magnificent fullness.

The Bible, especially the New Testament, is full of references to Holy Spirit—too many to put them all down on these pages. Here are a few just from the book of Galatians.

"Because you are sons, God sent the Spirit of his Son into our hearts, the Spirit who calls out, 'Abba, Father'" (Galatians 4:6). This is a great Trinitarian verse. Holy Spirit connects us to Father God and Jesus in an intimate way.

"So I say, live by the Spirit, and you will not gratify the desires of the sinful nature" (Galatians 5:16). What a great promise! We are called to "live by the Spirit."

"But the fruit of the Spirit is love, joy, peace, patience, kindness, goodness, faithfulness, gentleness and self-control" (Galatians 5:22). A great lifestyle!

"Since we live by the Spirit, let us keep in step with the Spirit" (Galatians 5:25). This is a very instructive verse. Christians are born again by the activity of the Holy Spirit and we enter into a dynamic relationship with God. We are then instructed to "keep in step with the Spirit." To a servant's ears that sounds like instruction leading toward service; to a son's ears (in close relationship with a great dad) that sounds like an invitation to adventure and participation in the family business of salvation and miracles.

Keeping in step with Holy Spirit is a daily invitation to adventure and destiny, an invitation to walk side by side with God Himself, just as the disciples did with Jesus. This is no meager substitute! This is the greatest privilege available on planet earth, and it is available to everyone who has been born again.

A life of righteousness, peace and joy in the Holy Spirit.

## The Father's Delight

I find it amazing that many Christians get nervous (maybe even anxious) about the activity of the Holy Spirit, and also about receiving Him. Jesus made it clear that our dear Father in heaven delights to give us the Holy Spirit.

> "Which of you fathers, if your son asks for a fish, will give him a snake instead? Or if he asks for an egg, will give him a scorpion? If you then, though you are evil, know how to give good gifts to

your children, how much more will your Father in heaven give the Holy Spirit to those who ask him!"

Luke 11:11–13

I have made it my determination over the years not to apologize for the activity of the Holy Spirit, but, rather, as best I can, to give scriptural explanations, similar to the way that Peter did on the Day of Pentecost.

> Then Peter stood up with the Eleven, raised his voice and addressed the crowd: "Fellow Jews and all of you who live in Jerusalem, let me explain this to you; listen carefully to what I say. These men are not drunk, as you suppose. It's only nine in the morning! No, this is what was spoken by the prophet Joel: 'In the last days, God says, I will pour out my Spirit on all people. Your sons and daughters will prophesy, your young men will see visions, your old men will dream dreams. Even on my servants, both men and women, I will pour out my Spirit in those days, and they will prophesy. I will show wonders in the heaven above and signs on the earth below, blood and fire and billows of smoke. The sun will be turned to darkness and the moon to blood before the coming of the great and glorious day of the Lord. And everyone who calls on the name of the Lord will be saved.'"
>
> Acts 2:14–21 (quoting Joel 2:28–32)

Physical manifestations often accompany the activity of the Holy Spirit, such as speaking in tongues, falling to the floor (the apostle John tells in the book of Revelation that he was "in the Spirit on the Lord's day," and when he heard the voice of Jesus he fell as though dead), prophecies, trances or visions—all of which we find in the Bible.

Why then do some Christians regard these things with suspicion, and, more than that, sometimes point to these manifestations as evidence of false signs and wonders?

It is time to learn to trust the Holy Spirit more and to grow in intimacy with Him.

It is time to unwrap the bonds of suspicion with regard to His activity.

It is time to unwrap the bonds of self-effort and learn to keep in step with the Spirit.

It is also time to cast off the idea of the Holy Spirit as anything less than Almighty God and welcome His activity in all its fullness.

One of my favorite Bible verses (I have many!) is Ephesians 1:17: "I keep asking that the God of our Lord Jesus Christ, the glorious Father, may give you the Spirit of wisdom and revelation, so that you may know him better."

Do you want to know Him better?

In the next few chapters we will look at some of the gems of truth contained within this verse.

## Unwrapping the Bonds

What is your relationship with God like? Are you relying more on self-effort or God's Spirit?

Are you comfortable calling Him by His name—Holy Spirit? Why or why not?

What difference has His coming made in your life?

# 8

# UNWRAPPING THE BIBLE

## Revealing the Invitation Within

One of them was called Cleopas.

We find him in Luke 24, walking along the road to Emmaus with someone else, whose name we do not know.

This is a story I love. I imagine myself listening to the inter-action between these two and the one who joins them—whom they fail to recognize. It takes place on the very day that Jesus has risen from the dead.

> Now that same day two of them were going to a village called Emmaus, about seven miles from Jerusalem. They were talking with each other about everything that had happened.
>
> Luke 24:13–14

We know very little about these two people. We can only guess as to the nature of their relationship—possibly husband

and wife, possibly friends, maybe relatives. It is fair to presume that they are followers of Jesus. Later in the passage they talk about "some women among us," so identifying themselves with the group of people who were close to Jesus and who had been so dramatically affected by His crucifixion.

They are walking from Jerusalem to Emmaus, a distance of about seven miles. We can presume once more that they are going home, as is indicated later in the passage when they extend an invitation to Jesus to "stay with us."

These two individuals are bound by unbelief. Their intellects and their experiences have not yet crossed the line of faith that grasps the truth of the promises about Jesus in Scripture. They do not believe what Jesus has said personally about His death and resurrection, and they refuse to believe the testimony of friends about the empty grave. How is Jesus going to unwrap their unbelief? Let's listen in.

## Trouble Believing

The two travelers on the road to Emmaus are talking about all the things that have taken place, trying to make sense of what they have witnessed, when someone joins them.

> As they talked and discussed these things with each other, Jesus himself came up and walked along with them; but they were kept from recognizing him. He asked them, "What are you discussing together as you walk along?" They stood still, their faces downcast.
>
> Luke 24:15–17

I love this part!

Jesus approaches them, starts to walk with them and somehow they are not able to recognize Him. I do not know how that works, but it interests me. Then Jesus enters the conversation, asking them what they are talking about. They stop in their tracks and sadness is all over them.

> One of them, named Cleopas, asked him, "Are you only a visitor to Jerusalem and do not know the things that have happened there in these days?"
> "What things?" he asked.
>
> Luke 24:18–19

They are surprised at this stranger. Who in Jerusalem could possibly be unaware of the arrest and brutal death of the one so hated by the religious hierarchy and so revered by the people?

I love the next bit, too. It really appeals to my sense of humor. "What things?" says Jesus, acting as if He is unaware; playing along; having fun.

> "About Jesus of Nazareth," they replied. "He was a prophet, powerful in word and deed before God and all the people. The chief priests and our rulers handed him over to be sentenced to death, and they crucified him."
>
> Luke 24:19–20

They give Jesus a short summary.

What they say is true, but it is not the full truth. Jesus was a prophet, but He is much more than that. He had been crucified, but now He is risen.

They had certain hopes about Jesus, but these were limited hopes—not taking in the full scale of God's intentions: "We had hoped that he was the one who was going to redeem Israel. And what is more, it is the third day since all this took place" (verse 21).

Jesus had taught them that He would die, and that on the third day He would rise again. They seem to acknowledge this intellectually, but it has never become an assured hope. Now, compounded by sorrow and bewilderment, their hope is at a low ebb. Faith is missing—the sort of faith that is the assurance of things hoped for and the certainty of things not yet seen (see Hebrews 11:1).

> "In addition, some of our women amazed us. They went to the tomb early this morning but didn't find his body. They came and told us that they had seen a vision of angels, who said he was alive. Then some of our companions went to the tomb and found it just as the women had said, but him they did not see."
>
> Luke 24:22–24

They confess that witnesses are confirming what Jesus told them would happen—or at least they have an angel's report about it (which you think would be reasonably convincing).

How much more do they need?

I believe the clue is in the last few words: *but Him they did not see.* It seems to me that they are saying, "We need to see *Him* to know that it's true."

## What About the Promises?

If we think of our everyday lives, many Christians, especially in the Western world, have plenty of knowledge about Jesus—mainly acquired through the Bible—but struggle with a lack of faith to believe all the promises contained within it.

Earlier I mentioned the impact of John 14:12 on me. It was in 2007, when I had been a Christian for more than thirty years and had been leading a church for almost twenty years, that I realized I did not really believe this promise. It came as a bit of a shock: "I tell you the truth, anyone who has faith in me will do what I have been doing. He will do even greater things than these, because I am going to the Father."

Really!

Could that be true?

I acknowledged that this verse was in the Bible, but I had learned not to believe it could be true. Doing the works of Jesus seemed beyond me and doing *greater* works somehow came close to blasphemy! The reason behind this was that partly, without knowing it, I had linked my identity with my activity. In my mind, doing His works seemed to make me His equal. This was unconscionable. He is God and I am Pete!

A good friend of mine confirmed my sense that we could not expect to do the works of Jesus because we are not Jesus. He then suggested, on the other hand, that we could achieve "greater" works because that simply meant "more" works. Put that way, it seemed entirely reasonable, since Jesus was just one person and we are many. This is probably another outcome of mistaken identity.

But then I saw somebody who believes this verse literally— and not only believes it, but does it. I heard him teach that such things are possible for all who have faith in Jesus. I was stirred inside. I remember saying to Kim, who was at the same meeting, "If that man is right, it changes everything."

Back home, I sat down and studied the passage for myself. Finally I understood that the Greek word for *greater* meant quality, not quantity.

It is true, but I had missed the truth.

My understanding of the Bible had been limited and, in some ways, incorrect. So I set off on a new life adventure, believing that I could do the works of Jesus and being determined to equip others to do the same. I was hungry to change and develop my Christian life to line up with the fullness of God's promises. It has been fun and challenging. I have some ideas about what greater works look like, but that will probably need to wait for another time.

In many ways, I had been like the two people on the road to Emmaus, acknowledging the truth of God's words but not living in their fullness. I knew Jesus, but I did not fully recognize Him. Our response of faith to God's words is what brings them into reality in our lives.

My experience tells me that God's grace is amazing and His loving voice is calling me forward into greater adventures of faith. He is taking me from where I am and leading me on.

## Where the Heart Figures In

This Bible story of the Emmaus road indicates again just how wonderful Jesus is. He interacts with these two in the context of their current understanding, knowing their great desire to see Him risen from the dead. He is about to turn their sadness into rejoicing, their hopelessness into hope and their doubt into radiant faith: "He said to them, 'How foolish you are, and how slow of heart to believe all that the prophets have spoken! Did not the Christ have to suffer these things and then enter his glory?'" (Luke 24:25–26).

Jesus tells them that they are foolish, which might seem to us to lack tact, but, in fact, is an example of speaking the truth in love. Jesus wants to lift them out of their folly and enable them to live unbound in the good of all that He has done and is going to do.

*"Slow of heart to believe."* Sometimes we think that doubt resides in our intellects—our rational minds struggling to come to terms with the unseen spiritual realm. We fix our eyes solely on the circumstances surrounding us, and let our rational minds explain away the promises of God.

Here Jesus is pointing out that doubt is a "heart condition"—an inclination of the heart to trust more in our own understanding than in the promises of God.

Proverbs 3:5 tells us to "trust in the Lord with all your heart and lean not on your own understanding." Depending upon my own understanding is like living in grave clothes, since my understanding is limited. Instead, the Bible instructs me to trust in God with all of my heart.

Like doubt, trust is also a heart issue more than an intellectual issue. Trust is rooted in relationship. The more I know someone, the more I know his character and abilities, the easier it is to trust him appropriately.

God is a perfect, infinite, eternal being. As I develop my relationship with Him, I grow in faith. My heart attitudes and leanings grow and line up with His revelation of Himself. Trusting Him is what Christian faith is all about.

So Jesus begins to open the eyes of their hearts. "And beginning with Moses and all the Prophets, he explained to them what was said in all the Scriptures concerning himself" (Luke 24:27). Jesus uses what we now call the Old Testament to explain to them about Himself. It must have been quite a lesson! In verse 32 we read that it affects them in such a way that their hearts are burning within them.

Imagine having a Bible study with Jesus!

How awesome!

And they are excited to understand the Scriptures better.

## They Finally See

But notice: Does this open their eyes? Does their understanding of the Scriptures enable them to recognize Jesus Himself? Does their understanding compel them to go and tell others about this wonderful truth? No. They do not yet recognize Him: "As they approached the village to which they were going, Jesus acted as if he were going farther. But they urged him strongly, 'Stay with us, for it is nearly evening; the day is almost over'" (Luke 24:28–29).

Again this amuses me. Jesus acts as if He is going to continue His journey along the road, leaving them to go inside their home and enjoy the recollection of an amazing Bible study.

But then comes what I believe is the pivotal moment in this story: They invite Him inside. Their world is about to be radically changed.

> So he went in to stay with them. When he was at the table with them, he took bread, gave thanks, broke it and began to give it to them. Then their eyes were opened and they recognized him, and he disappeared from their sight. They asked each other, "Were not our hearts burning within us while he talked with us on the road and opened the Scriptures to us?"
>
> Luke 24:29–32

Jesus responds to their invitation, and then He takes the initiative. Taking the bread He blesses and breaks it, and begins giving it to them. It is at this moment that revelation hits them, and they recognize Him.

I would like to suggest to you that Bible knowledge is important, but it does not guarantee full understanding and experience. Our knowledge of the Bible is meant to make us hungry for more revelation and experience of God Himself. We are not meant to satisfy ourselves with Bible knowledge, even if it does cause our hearts to burn. Rather, our Bible knowledge is meant to make us hungry for more of God, so that we invite Him to come in and be with us, where He can interact with us to reveal Himself to us in greater measure.

*Intimacy with God is the place where the revelation of God is most likely to happen.*

Our need for revelation is greater than our need for understanding.

Knowing about Jesus is no substitute for experience of Jesus.

Jesus wants us to invite Him continually into the innermost parts of our being. As we do so, the Holy Spirit of revelation will make Him more and more known to us; so that we can know Him better; so that we can truly recognize Him.

> They got up and returned at once to Jerusalem. There they found the Eleven and those with them, assembled together and saying, "It is true! The Lord has risen and has appeared to Simon." Then the two told what had happened on the way, and how Jesus was recognized by them when he broke the bread.
>
> Luke 24:33–35

Another outcome of this revelation of Jesus in their lives is the urgency to go and tell others the truth of their experience. The Bible study does not cause them to want to return to Jerusalem, but the revelation of Jesus does.

Christian leaders often wonder how they can motivate believers to want to tell others the Good News of Jesus Christ. We can run training sessions, preach sermons, organize courses—all of which can be good. But I would like to suggest to you that someone who has had an encounter with God and recognizes greater truth through that encounter will be better equipped and motivated because he or she has experienced personally the Good News.

When people get excited about God it shows!

The Holy Spirit brings revelation into our lives, and that changes us. In the next chapter we will look at some of the ways in which that can happen.

## Unwrapping the Bonds

If someone asked you whether or not the promises of the Bible are really true, what would you say?

How would you describe your "heart condition"? Do you depend on your mind in matters of the Spirit?

Why do you think these disciples' eyes were opened when Jesus broke the bread?

What is the Bible inviting you to do that you have hesitated to do?

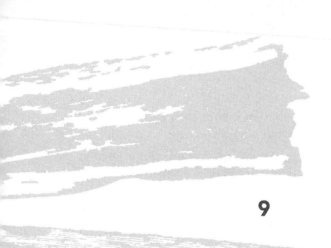

# 9

# UNWRAPPING IMAGINATION

*Revealing the Endless Delight of Discovery*

It is called theology.

*Theology* means literally "the knowledge of God," but it has become a word more related to the study of God and religion. I love studying my Bible and reading books that help me gain understanding. God speaks to me through the Bible, and He speaks to me in many other ways as well. I have pursued courses of theological study and have taught such courses, often finding that in my preparation to teach others I learn a lot for myself in the process.

But what is the purpose of my study?

Do I want to know more about God, or do I want to know Him personally in greater measure? Do I want to impress people with my theological knowledge, or do I want to grow deeper in my relationship with Him?

In June 2011, I attended a conference at Holy Trinity Brompton, that amazing church in London, home of the Alpha course, and home to a people of enormous grace and generosity. I was there for a conference and also hoping to connect with some specific people.

The first speaker was David Ford, a professor of theology at Cambridge University. I must admit, I was not sure what to expect of this learned man. As he started to speak I became enthralled and my heart started to rejoice. At the end of his talk, I made my way to the front of the church in order to ask him a question, because I wanted to make sure that I had understood him correctly.

I greeted him and thanked him for a wonderful message, and then I asked my question. "Can I confirm that you are saying you believe in a continually developing theology?"

"Certainly," he replied. "Otherwise it can't be God, but only our limited thoughts about Him."

I was so excited that I was not sure what to do next, except get my cup of coffee and mull things over.

For a couple of years prior to this, a way of thinking had been developing in my head (maybe I had been slow in my understanding for those years). If God is eternal and infinite, then there is no end to His being. This means that there is always more to discover about Him. If theology is about knowing Him, rather than just knowing *about* Him, then our theology should be ever developing.

Professor David Ford had just confirmed to me a truth that made Christianity even more exciting. The pursuit of God is the discovery of His divine nature—and there is no end to this most pleasurable journey.

Theology is not a closed box of belief, a systematic way of understanding God in a limited fashion. Theology is the pursuit of the knowledge of the Most High, leading to a relationship of unfathomable depths of love, joy, peace and other delights.

So how do we go about this adventure?

I believe that the story of the road to Emmaus helps us enormously. The Bible gives us a wealth of background information that can thrill our hearts, but that information is not meant to be the end of the story. The Bible gives us a taste so that we can ask for more and invite God into the intimate places of our lives. As we enter into intimacy, God will reveal Himself to us in greater measure.

This is one of the reasons why we need to unwrap our identity as sons and daughters of God—because that opens the route to intimacy in a way that is completely different from that which a servant experiences. The revelation of the Father heart of God that has been unfolding in world Christianity over the past twenty years or so is, in my mind, fundamental to receiving increasing revelation.

In 2009, a couple of years before that conference at Holy Trinity Brompton, Kim and I had the privilege of spending three months in Redding, California, where we became part of Bethel Church.

That adventure started with a quiet word from a close friend of mine, Dave Stevens. Our leadership team was away on a retreat, and we were discussing how to implement into church life some of the things that we were learning, including ideas from our numerous visits with the leaders of Bethel Church. Lunchtime was drawing near so we were bringing our discussion to an end when Dave, who had been sitting quietly thinking things through, asked me a question: "Have you ever thought about an extended visit to Bethel?"

I answered by saying that visiting Bethel was always a delight and staying for longer was always tempting, but my life was too full to contemplate an extended visit.

"I think you should go, and one month won't be long enough. I think you should go for three months."

To my surprise the rest of the leadership team responded almost immediately, saying they thought that was a message from God and, yes, Kim and I should go.

So convinced were they, they committed to funding the whole adventure out of their own finances (a few other friends joined in this amazing generosity). It was a stunning act of faith on their part, hearing from God and acting upon it.

So Kim and I set about clearing our calendar and on April 16, 2009, we said good-bye to our house for a while and set off on an adventure of faith. Interestingly, it was 32 years to the day since we had started another adventure—dating each other. We arrived at San Francisco airport, hired a car and set off for Redding, tuning the car radio to various stations trying to acclimatize ourselves to American culture.

Because of previous visits to Bethel, we already had some personal connections. One of the people we got to know was Judy Franklin. She has become a good friend to us. Judy has an extraordinary relationship with God, as you can discover in her book, co-written with Beni Johnson, *Experiencing the Heavenly Realm* (Destiny Image, 2011). I think her level of relationship with God is actually meant to be the "ordinary" level, but somehow most of us Christians have contented ourselves with a lesser level—and we have managed to persuade ourselves that this is all we can expect this side of heaven.

But 1 Corinthians 2:9 says: "It is written: 'No eye has seen, no ear has heard, no mind has conceived what God has prepared for those who love him.'"

Now, in my mind I had parked that verse in heaven, meaning that I saw this as something to look forward to after I died. God was preparing amazing things for me to see, hear and experience, and I looked forward to it. While I was here in my earthly existence, however, such things were not really to be expected. Well, maybe occasional flashes of revelation on a special day! Occasional encounters, of which I had experienced a few. But I should not expect too much!

I was guilty of not reading the Bible fully, for the passage goes on to say:

> But God has revealed it to us by his Spirit. The Spirit searches all things, even the deep things of God. For who among men knows the thoughts of a man except the man's spirit within him? In the same way no one knows the thoughts of God except the Spirit of God. We have not received the spirit of the world but the Spirit who is from God, that we may understand what God has freely given us. This is what we speak, not in words taught us by human wisdom but in words taught by the Spirit, expressing spiritual truths in spiritual words. The man without the Spirit does not accept the things that come from the Spirit of God, for they are foolishness to him, and he cannot understand them, because they are spiritually discerned. The spiritual man makes judgments about all things, but he himself is not subject to any man's judgment: "For who has known the mind of the Lord that he may instruct him?" But we have the mind of Christ.
>
> 1 Corinthians 2:10–16

"God has revealed it to us by His Spirit." That is not future tense. It means that such things are available to be revealed to us now, before we die—we do not have to wait!

And because God is infinite, there will still be plenty to discover after we die and enter the eternal realm—a never-ending adventure of discovery of the nature of God.

"We have received the Spirit of God that we may understand what God has freely given us." Holy Spirit will teach us all things, not simply in terms of our intellect, but in terms of our experience as well. We must not settle for the limitations of an intellectual relationship with, and understanding of, God.

God has freely given us all things and He has done this for our enjoyment. We are meant to enjoy Him! Christian maturity is best measured in terms of relationship with God rather than intellectual understanding.

## Faithful in Devotion

Before I tell you about our extraordinary visit with Judy, I want to mention the first time I got insight into this revelation. It was on a mission trip to Mexico.

During my numerous travels to that country, I had the privilege of visiting a church in a small village called El Bethi. It is a remote setting, the village having a population of about six hundred. Most of the people work on the land and live in basic, but comfortable accommodation.

The church has its own building, which is spacious and welcoming. On my first visit we were welcomed by Leonardo, one of the church leaders. "What time do we start?" I asked, with my English mindset.

"When the people arrive!" came the reply, which caused me to think.

As the sun started to set, people began to come to the building, direct from their work on the land where they had been tending and planting their crops. Now I understood a little better. I watched as people kept coming, walking across the fields, smiling and expectant. The worship started, simple yet passionate, faces upturned in adoration of God. More people arrived, the intensity of the worship growing.

*These people really do love God,* I thought to myself.

Prayers rang out as well—adoration and petition side by side. It was beautiful and inspiring.

We had come to preach to them, to try to help them, but I realized that I was really there to learn. My intellectual understanding of the Bible, out of which I could teach them, paled into insignificance in the light of their passion and relationship with God. I learned that many of these people had a low level of reading ability and could not study the Scriptures in depth. Yet they knew God in a way that challenged and provoked me.

After the meeting we talked with Leonardo and asked him how such a wonderful church had formed, discovering that their faith was known throughout the area and other churches were springing up in other villages.

His reply changed my life.

"The little we know we do," he said.

They were faithful to the level of revelation and understanding that they had.

*How much do I know?* I wondered. *And how much do I do?*

As I thought about this some more, I realized that although these people at El Bethi might have a limited knowledge of the Scriptures, because of a lack of reading skills, they actually knew God better than I did. Far from "knowing a little"—they knew God! I believe that in their intimate devotion to Him, He continued to reveal more of Himself to them. It then followed that they knew Him better and grew in devotion. And more than that, they were faithful with what they had been given.

There is a big difference between devotion to knowledge of the Bible and devotion to God Himself. Our knowledge of the Bible should cause us to hunger for God, lead us into intimacy and result in worship and eagerness to share the love of God with other people.

And so back to Judy.

## Imagination Unwrapped

A few weeks after our arrival in Redding, Judy invited us to her home for lunch. She has an unusual gift of being able to help people enter into amazing visionary encounters with Him—a bit like the apostle John, who said in Revelation 1:10, "On the Lord's Day I was in the Spirit." Or Peter in Acts 10 when he saw the vision of a sheet coming down from heaven. Thus, after eating we asked her to lead us into an encounter with God.

I was hungry for Him! I wanted Him to reveal more of Himself to me—and I wanted to learn from Judy.

I laid myself down on the floor, put a cushion under my head and got comfortable. There was some gentle music in the background. Judy suggested that we close our eyes and deliberately draw close to God. That was something I was used to doing, confident in His promise that if I draw close to Him, He will draw close to me.

She then suggested that we ask Jesus to show Himself to us, which I did (as did Kim). This took a bit of concentration on my part. Engaging my imagination and allowing the Holy Spirit to speak to me through that part of my brain was not a common experience for me, but I was not a complete stranger to this idea. I allow my imagination to give me inspiration in all sorts of areas of life, why not harness it more to experience God?

As I allowed the Holy Spirit to touch my mind, I could see Jesus seated on a horse far off in the distance, across what looked to me like a vast open field or prairie.

A little bit of explanation about me at this point will prove useful. I love sport, pretty much any sport. I enjoy playing sport, watching sport, reading about sport. I have, however, next to no interest in sports that involve horses.

But there was Jesus on a horse, far off in the distance.

Judy suggested that I ask Jesus to come closer, so I did. As I asked, the vision changed. Jesus started slowly to ride His horse toward me. As He drew closer, I could see that He was leading another horse behind Him by its reins.

He drew up close to me and said, "This one is for you!"

Now, that was a surprise!

"Jump on," He said.

Without hesitating I jumped up onto the horse's back. Somehow, I was surprisingly at ease.

"Follow Me," said Jesus and off we set, slowly walking our horses through the vast landscape.

All of a sudden the vision changed. We were no longer on horses and we were no longer on earth! We were up in the galaxies, stars all around us.

I have always enjoyed the night sky, gazing at the stars, giving my eyes time to adjust so that gradually more and more stars become visible. This is a special delight in places that have little light pollution. And here I was, in my vision, with Jesus, among the stars! No light pollution to take away from the amazing sight surrounding me. I was in awe. And I was thoroughly enjoying myself.

"Come with Me," said Jesus and we set off to explore. Brilliant colors surrounded us—planets, moons, asteroids, stars! All set against the amazing peaceful blackness.

After a while Jesus led me into what I can only describe as a tunnel in space. As we entered into this place it seemed as though we were surrounded by a circular wall of stars, each one radiant in its created glory. We went farther in, my mind trying to drink in what I was seeing. About halfway through the tunnel, Jesus turned to me and said, "I like it here. I made this place."

And suddenly I realized that He made all things for His pleasure. An abstract thought, read in the Bible, suddenly burst into multicolor reality. He really does take pleasure in what He has made, and He wants to include us in His joy.

Wow!

Jesus turned away and continued on down the tunnel. I followed, new realizations filling my mind, endless opportunities to enjoy the infinite nature of God opening up in front of me.

As we came out of the end of the tunnel, Jesus turned to me once again. He asked me, "What do you want to see next?"

This took little thought. "I would like to see a sunset," I replied.

"Which one?" Jesus asked. This confused me a little.

"I'm sorry, but I don't understand the question."

"Which one?"

"I'm sorry, but I still don't understand the question," I said, slightly bemused.

"Which one?" came the reply.

"I still don't understand."

"You have billions to choose from!" Jesus said.

And in an instant of revelation I understood. I had limited my thinking to my previous experience of the earth's sun, thinking that there was only one sun to enjoy—not considering the fact that there are billions of suns in the universe, each one with its own beauty to behold. Billions of sunsets to enjoy throughout eternity! All of a sudden I was overwhelmed by the enormity of God and His creation. The experience I was enjoying was opening my mind and soul to new levels of wonder and adoration.

So I asked Jesus to choose for me and off we went in my vision to enjoy the most amazing sunset together—whereabouts in the universe I do not know. It did not matter, I was with Jesus enjoying the wonders of His creation as He chose to show me.

After some time, Judy spoke and I opened my eyes. The world still looked the same around me, but my understanding of God had grown. My enjoyment of Him was greater, my expectation was stronger. Christianity had just become even more exciting.

We shared our experiences, Kim also having had a profound encounter with Jesus.

After experiencing something like this for the first time, many thoughts bombarded my mind. I was excited and thrilled, but my mind was full of questions. What was this visionary experience? Did it all come from God? What level of validity could I give it?

About a week later I was in a meeting where a woman was praying for me. Her voice was quiet, her prayers gentle. She knew nothing about me or my previous experiences. I was relaxed and not particularly expectant of anything extraordinary when, all of a sudden, she said to me in a quiet voice, "God wants you to know that He has a horse just for you."

I almost shot out of my seat.

She had just enabled me to validate my encounter with God.

Judy had told us that we can use our imaginations in this way anytime we want. Over the next few months, Kim and I both grew in our experience and understanding of God through unwrapping our imaginations. Since that time we have helped many other people to enjoy God in a similar way. It is simple to do and, to my mind, just requires a childlike faith, ready to embrace the wonders of the imagination God has given to us as a great gift.

I have shared the account of this experience with many friends. In all honesty, I think some decided that I had gone a "little strange"—as certainly this goes beyond the bounds of many people's Christian experience and understanding. It seems mystic. Or as one friend, a church leader, said to me, "But, Pete, that is just experience!"

Exactly.

Christianity is meant to be an experience, not merely a philosophy or an intellectual pursuit. Jesus was an experience to His disciples—a full-on experience! An experience that they did not understand. But they grew through that experience, as well as through teaching, observation and revelation. They unwrapped their imaginations, and He revealed more of Himself to them.

## Can I Trust My Imagination?

I have heard it said on many occasions, "That is just your imagination"—spoken in such a way as to cause me to mistrust that part of my mind. The sentiment behind such a statement is that our imaginations are likely to be fertile ground for deception, rather than a gift from God for our enlightenment and enjoyment. I believe this thought itself is a deception, effectively robbing us of wonderful opportunities to discover more of the delight of knowing God.

Certainly, it is possible for our imaginations to be used in such a way as to be unhelpful to us. Yet, the Bible teaches us that we are transformed by the renewing of our minds (see Romans 12:2), and that we destroy enemy strongholds by taking every thought captive (see 2 Corinthians 10:5). I believe that it is essential to recognize our imaginations as part of our God-given minds. We embrace the opportunities placed therein by renewing this part of the mind and taking it captive for God.

Think of dreams. They occur in the realm of imagination. They are common throughout the Bible. Creativity also starts in the imagination. Let's unwrap our imaginations for God and make them a fertile ground for the Holy Spirit to interact with us.

Some friends of mine have an eight-year-old son who suffers from autism. His parents attend our church's School of Supernatural Ministry. Over the past year, as they have prayed for him, and after a specific visit to the North Kent Community Church Healing Centre, he has changed remarkably. He has had his own encounters with God, and his understanding and faith have grown immeasurably. Not only this, but his behavior has changed so much that he now has a whole new outlook on life. He is looking forward to the possibility of returning to mainstream schooling instead of being in an isolated learning environment. The whole family is benefitting from the changes coming about in his life.

How has this happened? His parents have embraced the possibilities of a Spirit-filled life, open to encounters with God, and God has done the rest. This young boy has encountered God and experienced Him in a way in which words alone could not reach.

God is amazing.

Let's press into discovering more of Him.

It is time to take off the restrictive clothing that holds the intellectual pursuit of God above all else, and put on new clothes that embrace revelation, experience, study and encounter as equally valid parts of our experience of Him.

When our imaginations are free, the delight of discovery is endless.

## Unwrapping the Bonds

When you read the Bible, are you focused on learning about God or getting to know Him better?

Do you think you know Him well? Do you think He knows you well?

Are you willing to be on more intimate terms with Him, or does that make you nervous?

How comfortable are you with letting Jesus send your imagination soaring?

# 10

# UNWRAPPING HOPE

*Revealing the Power to Overcome Disappointment*

It was called "The Royal Liverpool Children's Hospital."

As is obvious from its name, this hospital was in Liverpool and its sole purpose was to treat sick children. It was a center of excellence, working alongside Alder Hey Children's Hospital, which is situated in another part of the city (and into which it was eventually absorbed). It had a particular level of expertise in pediatric cardiology (children with heart problems) and was a leading center for heart surgery on children.

I started to work there on August 1, 1985. Two days previously our daughter, Kerry, had been born, and David was two and a half years old. I found it difficult starting a new job in a new city and in a new specialty, especially as Kerry's birth was so recent. As I treated sick children at the hospital, I had to stop myself continually from considering how I would feel if it were one of my children in front of me. Emotional detachment was hard to come by.

The pressure of the job was enormous, both in terms of the hours worked and the number of children to be seen. I also faced a steep learning curve of treating children instead of adults, as well as coping with the emotional needs of parents and other relatives. It was very demanding.

I think there is little to compare in terms of emotional challenge than for parents to see their children suffering. It pulls on all the emotions, not only the difficult ones—there is also joy as children recover from illness and hope is fulfilled. It was humbling to receive so much gratitude from parents and grandparents for the part that I played in the process of bringing health to children and releasing hope and destiny for the future.

More difficult was receiving thanks for doing "everything you could," when the outcome was not that which was hoped for. It was an emotional roller coaster for all of us.

As I have already said, this hospital specialized in heart surgery for children. I had the responsibility of looking after the children before and after their procedures. I am not a surgeon and was not involved with the actual surgery. That was performed by some amazing people who were dedicating their lives to saving the lives of children with heart defects. Some of the surgery was well established, but a lot of the procedures were groundbreaking, establishing new techniques that were starting to give hope of life where previously only a premature death beckoned.

The surgeons were amazing people, pushing back the boundaries of expectation. Now, more than 25 years later, many of the surgical procedures they pioneered have become a routine part of medical practice. Children who previously would have died can now have a confident expectation of life.

I love the wonders of medical advance.

Back in 1985, however, much of the cardiac surgery performed on these children carried significant risk. As part of my job, I worked on the Intensive Care Unit with the children following their operations, as many of them fought for life. Some lost their battle. It was never easy.

Another part of my job was preparing children for their surgery. Actually, this was the most difficult part of all. I accompanied parents and their children en route to the operating room, arriving at the anesthetic room door and watching as these parents held their children and kissed them before saying good-bye, not knowing if they would see their children alive again. Entrusting themselves, their hopes and dreams to the skills of the anesthetists, surgeons and nurses, they would then turn away, usually with tears flowing, and I would accompany them in silence to a room where they could wait.

Most times the children came through surgery and went home to an improved life, but all too often there was a sadder outcome. Day in and day out the medical staff faced the possibility of the same upheaval—the pain of disappointment and seeming failure when a child died.

I found that six months of this emotional challenge was sufficient for me. At the end of that time, I moved into general practice and pursued my medical career in that new environment. For me that path had already been decided; I was not setting out for a working life in pediatrics. But the experience I gained was invaluable for my future working life.

But what would have happened if all the doctors involved in the care of these children had decided that the emotional challenge was too great for them? What if, faced with disappointment time and again, they turned away from this branch of medicine for a less demanding one?

The answer is that we would never have benefitted from the

advances they fought for. Some of the people I worked with during those six months continued to work at that frontier of medical advance for twenty or thirty years. The extraordinary has become the ordinary because of their courage and diligence. Heart transplants, for example, have become a normal part of the medical world in the last forty years. I remember hearing the news in 1967 of the first heart transplant being performed by Christiaan Barnard. It was a groundbreaking piece of surgery and medical care. Unfortunately, most people who had the early transplants died during the process or at best had a very limited life expectancy, but that is no longer the case. Great advances have been made.

The willingness of pioneering people to overcome disappointment with hope, courage and diligence is one of the major reasons that we enjoy the benefits of our modern world.

One of the greatest costs of being a pioneer is emotional. But without people who are willing to pay the emotional cost for advance, we would all be much the poorer in so many aspects of life.

I believe that this has great relevance to the Christian life. Romans 5:5 talks about hope that does not disappoint, which is vitally important for each one of us. We will face many disappointments in our lives. If we allow them to crush our hope we will live impoverished lives, devoid of the breakthroughs in faith that are awaiting us.

Faith is the assurance of things hoped for. Hope fuels faith and faith fuels hope. Each one of us is on the journey from faith to assurance. It is an emotionally charged journey where disappointments have to be faced and overcome. This is true in all aspects of Christianity, but especially true in the area of healing.

How do we cope with the disappointment of people (maybe ourselves) not being healed when they have been prayed for? How do we learn not to be crippled by disappointment? What will keep us pressing forward and not giving up?

The answer is the God who is love. He is my comforter, my strength, my hope. His love always hopes and never fails.

This love becomes more real to us the more we have time with God, allowing Him to comfort us, strengthen us and restore our hope and courage. Then we will be able to press on in endeavors of faith. We can also draw strength from others and move on together. There is strength in numbers (and danger in isolation!).

People the world over are pioneering the way in Christian advance and breakthrough. Particularly in terms of healing, advances are being made so that in years to come it will be a normal part of Christian life; people will be healed who previously had to continue living with their illnesses. In Africa there are reports of Christian mission into various places where it is becoming common for deaf people to start to hear and for blind people to see. In Mexico there are reports of more than two hundred people raised from the dead. In our own environment such reports are helping us to become more confident in God's healing power. In particular, we have seen many people set free from asthma and knee problems. We have seen some breakthroughs when praying for people with cancer, and we are looking for more.

The love and power of God demonstrated through the lives of Christians has the ability to transform the lives of individuals, cities, regions and nations. We have seen this in our own region as we reach out unconditionally to others.

We need to cheer such pioneers on and support them, even when disappointments occur. More than this we need to join in, adding our faith to theirs, so that the Kingdom of God can advance more rapidly.

Let us unwrap the bonds of disappointment. It is time to put on hope—hope that overcomes disappointment.

I will try to help you understand this further as we progress through the book.

## Unwrapping the Bonds

As you think about the great disappointments you faced in the past, did you find it hard to retain hope?

What caused you to doubt?

If you are in a challenging situation now, what can you do to strengthen your hope?

What does "hope that does not disappoint" mean to you?

Can you go to God with your pain? Why or why not?

Is there someone else whom you can encourage?

# 11

# UNWRAPPING WISDOM

*Revealing the Thinking of Heaven*

It is called wisdom.

Wisdom is important. So important that a whole book of the Bible is formed around it. The book of Proverbs is an amazing compilation of thoughts, sayings and statements aimed to help direct us in our thinking. The acquisition of wisdom is something to long for.

The Bible is also full of examples of people using this gift. Let's look at a few of them to see how we can unwrap wisdom to reveal the thinking of heaven when we need insight or direction.

## The Source of Godly Wisdom

In Acts 6, we read that the disciples face a delicate situation that needs a solution:

> In those days when the number of disciples was increasing, the Grecian Jews among them complained against the Hebraic Jews because their widows were being overlooked in the daily distribution of food. So the Twelve gathered all the disciples together and said, "It would not be right for us to neglect the ministry of the word of God in order to wait on tables. Brothers, choose seven men from among you who are known to be full of the Spirit and wisdom. We will turn this responsibility over to them and will give our attention to prayer and the ministry of the word."

> Acts 6:1–4

The church in Jerusalem is experiencing explosive growth from the Day of Pentecost onward. It is worth noting that many of the people who hear the "Pentecost sermon" given by Peter are not inhabitants of Jerusalem, but pilgrims who have come from other lands. "God-fearing Jews from every nation under heaven" is how Acts 2:5 puts it.

Many of these people respond to the Good News of Jesus— three thousand on the first day alone and many more after. It appears that a good number decide not to go home, but to stay in Jerusalem and be a part of this new community of vibrant believers, gathering around the teaching of the apostles, praying and worshiping together, seeing miracles and pooling their resources so that needs are met. Some even sell property to support this developing family of believers.

What an amazing church to be part of!

But with any growing church or organization, the infrastructure has to change and develop as things move along, and it is not uncommon for something to get overlooked. In this case, the Grecian widows are missing out on the daily distribution of food. We are not told how this situation comes about, but a solution needs to be found.

120

The twelve apostles face an interesting and important decision about their priorities. How best should they use their time?

This is a situation that is repeated in every church year by year—how should people prioritize their time? And not only in church. To my mind, this is one of the most important questions in life. Time is the one thing you cannot get more of; it is the most precious commodity.

The apostles decide that they must not neglect their God-given calling in order to help meet the pressing need of feeding everybody, but they do not neglect the need either. They come up with a solution to the problem: delegation. This is a good solution in any church.

Whom shall they delegate this responsibility to? The apostles set two criteria for the selection of people suited to the task: The people must be known to be full of the Spirit and wisdom.

I believe the order of these two is important. In order to live the Christian life as Jesus and the Father intend, we need to be full of the Holy Spirit continuously. The Holy Spirit is not an optional extra!

Reading this passage in Acts, it is clear that people can recognize others who are full of the Spirit. As 1 Corinthians 12:7 says, "Now to each one the manifestation of the Spirit is given for the common good." In other words, one of the ways the activity of Holy Spirit is obvious is the benefit He brings to the community of believers. The early Church is so dependent on Holy Spirit and in tune with Him, they can discern His activity easily. They are truly "led by the Spirit," being directed into all truth and into their mission. This makes the second criteria for service easily discernible within their numbers: wisdom.

How about us in our modern-day churches and our modern-day lives?

Is Holy Spirit's activity obvious to us?

Do we recognize God-given wisdom?

This is something that is exercising my brain a lot these days, particularly as I ponder certain verses. Are there sources of wisdom other than heaven?

Yes.

## A Dangerous Source of Wisdom

Here is a passage from the book of James that has provoked my thinking about where our wisdom comes from.

> Who is wise and understanding among you? Let him show it by his good life, by deeds done in the humility that comes from wisdom. But if you harbor bitter envy and selfish ambition in your hearts, do not boast about it or deny the truth. Such "wisdom" does not come down from heaven but is earthly, unspiritual, of the devil. For where you have envy and selfish ambition, there you find disorder and every evil practice. But the wisdom that comes from heaven is first of all pure; then peace-loving, considerate, submissive, full of mercy and good fruit, impartial and sincere. Peacemakers who sow in peace raise a harvest of righteousness.
>
> James 3:13–18

Verse 15 tells us that there is wisdom that does not come down from heaven. It comes, in fact, from a different source entirely: It is inspired by the devil!

Now that is a shock! It makes me seriously consider where my wisdom is coming from. Other Bible passages come to mind.

> The Spirit clearly says that in later times some will abandon the faith and follow deceiving spirits and things taught by demons. Such teachings come through hypocritical liars, whose consciences have been seared as with a hot iron. They forbid people to marry and order them to abstain from certain foods,

which God created to be received with thanksgiving by those who believe and who know the truth. For everything God created is good, and nothing is to be rejected if it is received with thanksgiving, because it is consecrated by the word of God and prayer.

1 Timothy 4:1–5

Demons like to teach! They have a doctrine of their own. Any teaching that takes us away from the grace of God and causes us to rely on our own works and righteousness, independent of the Holy Spirit, will lead us away from the truth of the Gospel.

When Paul confronts Peter, as outlined in the book of Galatians, he accuses him of not acting in line with the truth of the Gospel (see Galatians 2:14). In Galatians 3:1–5, Paul seeks to settle the issue by asking one question: How do Christians receive the Spirit: by observing the Law or by believing what they have heard?

Salvation comes through faith alone. In the same way the Holy Spirit comes through faith alone. We receive Him by faith not by works.

My experience and study have shown me that a large part of the devil's strategy is to try and take us away from our dependence on God (not much has changed in that respect since the Garden of Eden). He sets up strongholds that are designed to come against our knowledge of God—not simply intellectual knowledge, but more importantly intimate knowledge.

Strongholds are ways of thinking that exert a strong grip on us. The Bible tells us that the way to defeat enemy strongholds is by taking every thought captive and making it obedient to Christ (see 2 Corinthians 10:5).

In Matthew 16 we find an interesting account of a verbal exchange between Jesus and Peter:

From that time on Jesus began to explain to his disciples that he must go to Jerusalem and suffer many things at the hands of the elders, chief priests and teachers of the law, and that he must be killed and on the third day be raised to life.

Peter took him aside and began to rebuke him. "Never, Lord!" he said. "This shall never happen to you!"

Jesus turned and said to Peter, "Get behind me, Satan! You are a stumbling block to me; you do not have in mind the things of God, but the things of men."

Matthew 16:21–23

Jesus explains the plan of heaven for the salvation of the world. With the advantage of hindsight we understand what He is saying; it makes sense to us. Peter does not have this advantage, so he applies his thinking to the matter. He rebukes Jesus for considering such a course of action. The problem is, he does not have the mind of God on this; he is using human logic and wisdom. His thinking is not being directed by God, and he gets it badly wrong. So wrong that Jesus says, *Get behind Me, Satan!* Jesus attributes Peter's thoughts to a source entirely different from God!

It is easy to regard temptation merely in terms of being tempted to do something wrong or sinful. More subtle and perhaps even more dangerous is to allow our thinking to become influenced by the devil's strategies, allowing him to establish strongholds of thinking in our minds. Over the course of time, if such thinking goes unchecked, it will appear to us as wisdom.

Here are five tests to help you uncover the devil's subtle temptations to embrace wisdom that is "earthly, unspiritual, of the devil." Remember, 2 Corinthians 11:14 tells us that "Satan himself masquerades as an angel of light." He will try to convince us that his ways are enlightened. The truth is that they will lead us into darkness.

### The Presence of Fear

One of the best and simplest testing grounds for discerning that the devil is the source of the wisdom being offered is the presence of fear.

Let me give you an example. Many people think that caution is wisdom. This is not a concept that I can find in the Bible. The Bible does use the word *careful* a number of times, but it is generally used in a positive way, urging us to be careful to do all that God has placed in front of us. There is a big difference between being *careful*, in other words, taking care as we go about God's work, and being *cautious*, which often leads to inactivity. Caution has fear at its root, and the Bible clearly tells us that God has not given us a spirit of fear.

Simply put, any wisdom that has fear at its root does not come from God.

### The Lack of Freedom

Another testing ground to help you discern if the source of wisdom is "earthly, unspiritual, of the devil" has to do with freedom. Wisdom that removes freedom is contrary to the Gospel. Galatians 5:1 tells us that it is "for freedom that Christ has set us free."

As a church leader I know how difficult it can be to lead free people, particularly if I want to get them to do what I want! It is much easier to lead through rules and regulations. Many times over the years I have been tempted to lead in ways that will be humanly effective, but spiritually damaging. I have endeavored to resist this temptation because heaven's thinking is better than my own.

Here is an example. One of the challenges faced regularly by church leaders is the prayer life of their churches. I have heard many talks about the importance of prayer. Everyone agrees that prayer is important. We affirm slogans like, "A church that prays together stays together."

I once heard someone say that the size of your church is, in reality, related to the size of your prayer meeting. That thought would immediately discourage most church leaders I know! So we might consider a more encouraging thought from a different source: "You are doing well if 10 percent of your church attends your prayer meetings." Suddenly most of us felt more encouraged.

But is either way a good way to think?

Behind both sentiments is a philosophy that "getting people to prayer meetings is important"—which I am not necessarily contesting. But what if the method of getting them there, even if it is effective, violates their freedom?

A pastor might, for instance, try to get people to prayer meetings by making them feel guilty for not being there. I would suggest to you that this is a route of earthly wisdom that will ultimately lead to bad fruit, no matter how many people attend the meeting. Projecting guilt is not part of God's thinking. The Bible tells us that there is no condemnation in Christ Jesus.

At North Kent Community Church, we endeavor to lead people in freedom. We have tried to create an environment of freedom. In this environment people are free to enjoy God and each other. We do not try to control people or their choices. We believe that when people love Jesus and other people unconditionally, the overflow into the life of the church and the communities around us will be abundant. Freedom produces life and creativity, and it is from this that we believe effective prayer and evangelism will flow. Guilt and condemnation can produce compliance, but the fruit will be different from that produced in freedom.

We believe that God not only sets us free from things that would hold us back, but also makes us free to become all that He intends for us—free to pursue God-given dreams and free to be great in the Kingdom of heaven.

Freedom is part of heavenly wisdom. You can see this clearly in the account of Creation at the beginning of the book of Genesis. Throughout history a question has been asked: If God knew that sin would come into the world through the choice of Adam and Eve to eat the fruit of the Tree of the Knowledge of Good and Evil, why did He allow it?

Some strains of human logic conclude that God made an error. Somehow He should have ensured that sin was not possible. But heavenly wisdom values freedom so highly that sin was possible in a perfect creation. God created human beings with the freedom to make choices—even bad ones!

More about freedom in a later chapter.

### Not Getting Our Way

The Bible says in the James passage written above that earthly, unspiritual wisdom is often characterized by selfish ambition and bitter envy. A testing ground in this battle for our thinking is how we cope with disappointments—how we react when something does not work out the way we want it to.

Imagine that you have been praying steadfastly for a friend to be healed and as yet healing has not happened. Then someone else prays for that friend of yours for the first time, and healing occurs instantly. What will go through your head? What thoughts will rise to the surface? Will those thoughts be centered on rejoicing that your friend has been healed or disappointment because it did not happen when you were praying?

Another example: You have ambition for leadership in your church, which is a good thing. An opportunity for training arises, but a close friend is chosen instead of you. How do you feel?

We talked in the last chapter about hope and disappointment—these are common in life. How you process that disappointment is one of the keys to advancing in heavenly wisdom. Resisting the temptation to become jealous and bitter will open you to greater revelation of heavenly wisdom.

Frustration is similar—a common occurrence that is an opportunity for growth in patience and wisdom, or the development of bad attitudes.

I sometimes wonder how I would have responded if I had been one of the twelve disciples chosen by Jesus, but then not one of the three who went up the Mount of Transfiguration. Opportunities for disappointment and frustration knock on the door on a regular basis. The decision to open the door and welcome them in is within our own control.

Ephesians 6:16 says, "In addition to all this, take up the shield of faith, with which you can extinguish all the flaming arrows of the evil one." I believe that earthly wisdom is one of those flaming arrows. For too long we have welcomed it as a friend rather than repelled it with faith.

Let me give you an example. In recent years, Bible teaching has been coming forth from different sources relating to this section in the Lord's Prayer: "Your Kingdom come, Your will be done on earth as it is in heaven."

Expectation is arising within the Body that heaven can be expressed here on earth. This is resulting in increased expectation of miracles, and healing in particular. This has had a profound impact upon me; I believe it has led me into greater faith. The result in North Kent Community Church has been many more miracles and healings. Our faith is rising.

The question can rightly be asked: How much of heaven can

we expect here and now? My answer: More than I currently experience!

It surprises me, then, to hear church leaders teach against this possibility. Their thinking goes like this: If you lead people to expect too much, they will inevitably get disappointed. Consider healing. How do people cope with not being healed? If we expect more, there will be more disappointment. So we need to limit our expectations so as not to cause people emotional pain and difficulty.

This sounds reasonable in one sense, but does this thinking line up with the Bible?

It appears to me that such teaching has, at its root, fear of disappointment. The Bible teaches, remember, that God has not given us a spirit of fear. Romans 5:3–5 explains that difficulties produce perseverance, perseverance produces character, character produces hope, and this sort of hope will not disappoint us. Biblical hope will not produce disappointment; in fact, it will overcome disappointment.

So if we try to limit people's hope because we fear their disappointment, we are limiting their opportunity to grow in faith and hope. Heaven's wisdom will produce faith, not fear.

### A Negative, Cynical Attitude

Another testing ground for wisdom that is "earthly, unspiritual, of the devil" is cynicism. This is generally a negative attitude that views things with suspicion in the first instance. It has elements of superiority and arrogance within it, believing that one's own opinion is the most reliable and dismissing optimism as unrealistic. It can also carry a sense of judgment of other people's thoughts or actions. I am amazed that so many people think that suspicion is a friend to be welcomed into their lives. It promotes cynicism, negativity and a judgmental attitude.

When people ask you to "be real," is it an invitation to optimism or pessimism? Is the glass half-full or half-empty? Both can be the correct answer, but what attitude is underlying?

Sometimes when I read the Bible, I wonder if God has the same Bible as I have! Hebrews 11:32, for instance, includes Samson as one of the great heroes of faith. *That* Samson? The one who made so many mistakes, who gave in to Delilah and had his eyes gouged out? Yes, that Samson!

What is God's perception of Samson? A hero. Surely God's glass is half-full!

Similarly, look at the account of Abraham in Romans 4. There is no mention of his mistakes, just a recounting of his great faith. Heaven's perspective is in no way cynical; however, we can sometimes find ourselves cynical about heaven's perspective.

Cynicism does not produce faith. Rather, I believe that it is another flaming arrow that we need to extinguish by faith. This kind of rational pragmatism, which does not result in increased faith, needs to be resisted.

One of the ways we at North Kent Community Church have found most effective in combating this is developing a "good news culture," where we encourage and celebrate the sharing of good news. In this way, we are training and transforming our minds to be more in line with heaven's perspective.

Training ourselves and our thinking in this way is especially effective and is very much in line with what the Bible tells us in Philippians 4.

> Finally, brothers, whatever is true, whatever is noble, whatever is right, whatever is pure, whatever is lovely, whatever is admirable— if anything is excellent or praiseworthy—think about such things.
>
> Philippians 4:8

Heaven's wisdom concentrates on the good.

### False Humility

A final testing ground for wisdom that is "of the devil" is the presence of false humility rather than true humility. The Bible tells us that Jesus is humble, and that provides us with a clear picture of true humility. Such humility does not deny what God has made us to be and what He has called us to do. False humility, in contrast, will lead us to deny the magnitude of our God-given identity and our God-given calling.

"Greater works? Surely not!"

Jesus was secure in His identity and not afraid to proclaim His mission on earth. He stated that He is the Way, the Truth and the Life—the only way to the Father. That might not sound like a humble statement to ears that are accustomed to false humility, but it is a true statement. Truth and humility go hand in hand. True humility enables us to fulfill our callings. False humility needs to be resisted as it will be a hindrance to us.

As we have seen, the Kingdom of heaven should have priority in our thinking. Putting the Kingdom first helps us attain heavenly wisdom. It helps us overcome the dangers of comparison and competition between churches and individuals, combating the jealousy and misplaced ambition that can prevent us from rejoicing in other people's success. It places us in a context where we have plenty to rejoice about and in which any endeavor of faith plays a part in the advance of God's purposes.

## Evidence of Heaven's Thinking

As we seek to unwrap the wisdom that comes from heaven for our benefit, we need to try to ensure that we recognize "earthly wisdom" so that we can avoid being bound by or entangled in it. Below I have given some pointers to help.

James 3 tells us that "heavenly wisdom is pure." My favorite definition of *purity* is "the quality of being uncontaminated." Below is a list of some of the things that I believe wisdom from heaven cannot be contaminated by (we have discussed several of these):

| | |
|---|---|
| Fear | Bitterness |
| Unbelief | Discord |
| Loss of freedom | Unforgiveness |
| Suspicion | Dishonesty |
| Selfish ambition | Cynicism |
| Jealousy | Judgmental attitudes |
| Hatred | False humility |

What place, if any, do these things have in my personal life, the life of my church community and other contexts in which I find myself? Let us unwrap such things from our lives and seek instead to be clothed in the pure wisdom of heaven.

Heavenly wisdom is:

| | |
|---|---|
| Peace loving | Full of mercy |
| Considerate | Productive of good fruit |
| Unselfish | Impartial |
| Submissive | Without hypocrisy |
| Humble | Full of love |

## Unwrapping the Bonds

How can you recognize God-given wisdom?
Why might the devil's wisdom sound convincing?

Which of the five ways that the devil imposes his wisdom (as discussed in this chapter) is the most likely to seem like "light" to you? What are you doing to safeguard yourself against it?

Which aspects of heavenly wisdom (list given above) are easiest for you to recognize?

Does it feel like false humility to believe that you are clothed with some of these characteristics of heavenly wisdom?

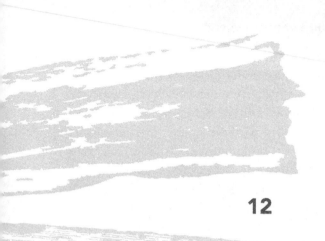

# 12

# UNWRAPPING AUTHORITY

## *Revealing Access to Resources*

As a medical student I was excited by the idea of helping in a crisis. Watching doctors respond to their beeper/pagers, having been called upon to intervene in life-and-death situations, was appealing. The sense of being needed and valued played to my sense of pride and destiny.

Being around when a cardiac arrest call went off meant getting caught up in a flurry of activity, as doctors sprinted along hospital corridors, white coats flapping, dodging anything or anyone in the way of their rapid progress. All this in order to get to the patient as quickly as possible and try to restore life. As a medical student, of course, I was only an observer. I witnessed this only on rare occasions. It seemed so dramatic and fulfilling.

I was looking forward to having my own beeper/pager and being called into action in my own right as part of a team saving lives, being instantly available to come to the aid of someone in need.

On June 18, 1982, my life changed. I took my final examinations as a medical student, thankfully passed, and became a doctor.

I was now Dr. Peter Carter, M.B., Ch.B. I was registered with the General Medical Council of Great Britain. I had authority to access all the resources of the National Health Service for the benefit of my patients.

On August 1, 1982, reality struck.

## Authority Under Pressure

It was a Sunday and the first day of my working life as a qualified doctor. Having inquired beforehand, I knew that I had to start my day on the Intensive Care Unit. Quite a start! On Sundays the normal complement of medical staff was not in the hospital: only those "on call," and one of them was . . . me!

I was part of a small team of doctors "covering" the hospital. In other words, anything that needed the attention of a doctor would come our way. For me that meant I was first in line for any medical emergency admissions or problems with the 120 patients on the adult medical wards (as opposed to surgical wards). I was also part of the cardiac arrest team when I was on call. Along with two other doctors I had to be ready during those hours to respond instantly to any cardiac arrest situation in the entire hospital.

In order to fulfill these duties I needed to carry my own personal beeper and also a cardiac arrest beeper. Having collected these precious items, I made my way to the Intensive Therapy Unit to start my medical career. I guess I had a sense of self-importance and prestige as I stepped onto the ward, knowing that I was needed and would be in demand. Nurses would want my help because they did not have the authority to prescribe drugs, order investigations and do all sorts of other things.

The problem was, I did not have any experience of handling such demand and authority. I had never been placed under that much pressure and I was not familiar with the working practices of that particular hospital.

One other doctor in my team of three was also new to the hospital. Fortunately, a senior doctor was there at the beginning of the workday. The senior doctor took charge, and we went to see each patient on the Intensive Therapy Unit in turn. He assessed the situation and gave us instructions about changes in medications, investigations to order and what was required for each patient. The nursing staff on the ITU were friendly, efficient and helpful. Things seemed to be going well.

At the end of our ward round on ITU, the senior doctor informed us that he would be available at home if we needed him!

My mind started to process things quickly. During my training as a medical student I had been working in large teaching hospitals where there were always lots of staff around, and I guess that had been my expectation. Here in a provincial hospital with much fewer staff I suddenly realized that there were only going to be a few people around to help me. The senior doctor walked off the ward and left me and the other doctor, only slightly more experienced than I, alone to face whatever came our way.

Then my beeper sounded. The thing I had anticipated for three years suddenly brought a new sense into my life—immense responsibility and pressure. I was needed on one of the other wards to review certain patients.

"Can you make it as soon as possible?" I was asked.

"Certainly," I replied and set off.

En route my beeper sounded again (this was an era before mobile phones) so the first task on getting to my destination was to pick up a phone and discover that I was needed in another ward where a patient was looking ill.

What should I do first?

I decided to start on the ward that had called me first as I was already there.

Shortly after this my beeper sounded again. I was needed to re-site an intravenous line, "urgently please," as the patient needed drugs administered by that route.

Fortunately, after this flurry the beeper grew still for a little while, enabling me to get through much of my work list. Then came calls telling me to expect the arrival of emergencies into the hospital, new patients who would need careful attention.

The beeper continued to summon me throughout the 24 hours that I was on call, my head turning dizzy with the weight of expectation suddenly placed upon me.

I came to realize that with authority came responsibility, and with responsibility came pressure.

To my recollection, during that first 24 hours of my medical career, the cardiac arrest bleep sounded twice, a rapid succession of high-pitched sounds summoning me to respond instantly. All the staff around were aware of that sound and what it meant. Dropping everything, I ran to the patient who needed to be resuscitated; this carried priority over everything else.

At the end of the 24 hours I was happy to hand over the cardiac arrest beeper to someone else who would take up the position on the front line between life and death, knowing that every third day and weekend I would receive it once again. Between those times I carried my personal beeper, which continued to summon me on a frequent basis.

It was a steep learning curve, facing priorities, choices, pressure, the elation of victory over illness and the disappointment when our efforts could not overcome the progression of sickness.

I remember the first complete weekend I served on call (72

hours without respite, grabbing an hour or so of sleep when possible). On the Saturday night, during the hours of midnight and eight a.m. when I was trying to get some sleep, I had to respond to seven emergency calls, wearily dragging my tired body out of bed and into action, calling on God to strengthen me so that my patients would get the best Dr. Carter available, rather than the exhausted version.

To be honest, during that first month I wondered why I had wanted to become a doctor. The pressure was enormous, the weight of expectation almost crushing and the tiredness overwhelming. The sense of needing to learn quickly was also acute. After the first month, however, I started to enjoy myself. I grew into the job and began to be at ease with the sense of responsibility and authority. I learned what was important, what was urgent and what could wait. Sometimes there were things that simply would not get done as they were neither important nor urgent in the grand scheme of medical care.

That month of August 1982 was probably the most intense learning period of my life. The lessons I learned there and subsequently in my medical career, have stood me in good stead throughout life, especially in regard to the nature of authority and how it should be used. Although I had authority, I lacked experience. I soon realized that in many situations the nurses knew more than I did, so I regularly asked them the question, "What do we normally do now?" They guided me in the right direction and helped me to learn much more quickly. We worked as a team and as a result the patients received better care.

## Wrong and Right Uses of Authority

As my medical career developed, I became one of the senior doctors on the medical team in the hospital where I was working.

I was placed in charge of the cardiac arrest team when I was on call. This meant that I took charge of the situation, and the team worked under my instructions. In such a situation there was no discussion with other members of the team (or indeed with the patient), but rather everyone followed my instructions without question and without delay. This was necessary to give us the best chance of a positive outcome, since any delay could be detrimental. Time was of the essence. I got used to reacting to emergency situations and taking control.

During this time, my first six months working in the hospital, our son, David, was born. In fact, we found out that Kim was pregnant with him the same day that I passed my final examinations in medical school. (Life really did change that day!)

Needless to say, I was keen for David to be healthy and was happy that he would benefit from my medical knowledge. As he grew and learned to walk and run, inevitably from time to time he fell over and hurt himself. If I was present, I would immediately put myself in emergency mode (for his benefit, of course!). I remember barking orders to Kim as to what I wanted her to do, as I took charge of the situation. This, however, did not go down well. Kim did not appreciate being ordered around in this fashion, whereas I saw it as normal.

I was overreacting. I expected Kim to respond in emergency mode as part of my team. Often the only "resources" needed were a cuddle, some comfort and maybe a dressing on the cut or scrape. This was not a cardiac arrest! This mode of using authority was inappropriate in this context.

As a practicing physician in the U.K., I have authority to access the resources of the National Health Service for the benefit of my patients. I use my knowledge and experience to direct them to appropriate treatments relevant to their medical condition.

One of the key principles involved is the principle of informed consent. This means that I have a responsibility to inform my patients of the benefits and risks of a certain form of treatment so that they can make an informed decision as to whether they want to accept that treatment. It would be an abuse of my authority to insist on treatment without consent.

In a cardiac arrest situation, however, there is no informed consent, no discussion with the patient about the pros and cons of different options, not even discussion with the rest of the team, just hectic activity aimed at restoring life. In that situation authority is used in a certain way, but it is not a model for how to use it in the rest of life.

This scene comes to mind in this regard. A middle-aged gentleman was brought by ambulance to the Accident and Emergency Department ("emergency room" in the United States). He was suffering a heart attack that was threatening his life. Though conscious and able to converse in a limited way, he was in severe pain and distress. In this situation I introduced myself as the doctor responsible for him and told him that we needed to run some tests and do some things to help him. It was an emergency so we needed to do things quickly, such as setting up an intravenous line, taking blood for various tests, performing an electrocardiogram and setting up a heart monitor.

The team of doctors and nurses were well practiced in these things and worked with calm efficiency, performing their various tasks so that things got done quickly, talking to one another and passing on information. The patient was the recipient of excellent care, but in reality there was no informed consent from him. He was in too much pain and shock to understand the intricacies of all that was happening and was more interested in being relieved of his pain and taken out of danger than anything else. This was an emergency, where the threat to life and the alleviation of pain were the top priorities. This man was happy to trust that we knew best and that we would use our knowledge, expertise and resources for his benefit. He did not want to discuss the details of what was happening to him at that time. I am pleased to say that he recovered well.

During his recovery we wanted to arrange further investigations, which would benefit him but which also carried a risk. Now that he was out of pain, in a stable condition and at ease in his mind, I was able to talk with him about the proposed procedure, the benefits and the risks, in such a way that he could understand and give his informed consent if he wished. He gave his consent to the investigation and to the cardiac surgery that followed as a result of the findings and went on to make an excellent recovery and return to health.

I enjoyed working in a hospital, but in the end decided that my long-term career would be as a general practitioner. So I did the necessary training and found myself a place in general practice as a partner in a busy medical center. In general practice most of the work cannot be classified as emergencies. It is far more about helping people to live as healthfully as possible for themselves, overcoming illness and, where it cannot be overcome entirely, managing it in the optimum way.

My job is really one of dispensing appropriate health advice to individuals and families in their particular contexts. In order to do that, I endeavor to help my patients understand as much as possible about their illnesses, treatment options and when treatment is not necessary. I want to help people understand that their personal health is their personal responsibility. They retain authority over their bodies and for their health. I do not believe that I have authority over somebody else's health or his life. Rather, I believe that I have authority from the British government in order to access the resources of the health service for the benefit of my patients in line with their informed consent.

It takes extreme situations, such as a cardiac arrest, other causes of imminent death, criminal behavior or psychiatric illness so severe that the person presents a danger to himself or others, in order for it to be valid for me to work outside the boundaries of informed consent and take authority over an individual's situation.

## The Reason for Authority

I believe these principles from the medical world carry forward into life in general. Normal life is not an emergency, so to try and exercise authority over other people rather than for them goes beyond normal boundaries. People have authority over their own lives.

Obviously there are different models of how authority works in different contexts. The military, for example, have a clearly defined authority structure appropriate for their work, as do the police. Consider teachers. What authority do they have over pupils? How do they use their authority for the benefit of the class as a whole as well as for individual students?

These are complex questions.

But underlying all these things I have a core belief that *when authority is given to you it should result in the benefit of others.*

Authority is not a means of self-promotion. The outcome of the correct use of authority and its attendant resources should be freedom in all its guises.

As a doctor I work toward the end that people will be free from sickness and pain. The police work toward the end that there will be freedom in society from crime and disorder. Teachers work toward the aim that their students will have an education, making them free to fulfill their potential.

Any use of authority that reduces people's freedom needs to be put under scrutiny.

Obviously in society there is a need for measures that limit the freedom of people to do things that could be damaging to other people and society as a whole—that is why we have a legal system and prisons. The use of such authority should increase freedom in society.

## Kingdom Resources

In this chapter I have been trying to describe various ways in which people exercise authority. I hope you will be able to recognize these from your own experiences. I have tried to illustrate from my medical background how I have exercised authority in different ways in different contexts, and also how the incorrect use of authority is unhelpful.

I believe that it is important to exercise authority correctly according to the circumstance. This leads to a question: How is authority used in the Kingdom of God? What model should we look at to help us? Let me provide a short summary of my thinking.

Christians have been given authority by Jesus in order to do the works that He did and even greater works. I believe that all Christians have been given authority by God in order to access the resources of heaven for the benefit of the world around them. The use of godly authority by Christians should be in line with the character of God Himself. The fruit of the Spirit give us a good checklist for how we are meant to behave toward others and give us a context for the use of authority.

Authority should be used in a way that reflects love, joy, peace, patience, kindness, goodness, faithfulness, gentleness and self-control. Not only should it reflect these things, it should produce them as its own fruit. When looking for the best example of how godly authority works we need to look no further than Jesus Himself. How did Jesus use authority? In the next chapter we will look into the gospels to learn more about this important subject.

One quick thought before we press on. I perceive that Jesus used His authority to serve others. Most of the time He did this by demonstrating the Kingdom of heaven positively. Sometimes, however, this took the form of opposing religious thinking and structures, removing unhelpful blocks so that people could experience God. In Matthew 23:13 Jesus said, "Woe to you, teachers of the law and Pharisees, you hypocrites! You shut the kingdom of heaven in men's faces. You yourselves do not enter, nor will you let those enter who are trying to."

Jesus opposed people who stood in the way of others entering the Kingdom of heaven. When He cleared the Temple, it was an example of this.

When Jesus gave authority to His disciples, He instructed them to use such authority to demonstrate and preach about the Kingdom of heaven. If they were rejected, He instructed them to move on to another place and try again.

Our main focus should not be to oppose other people, but rather to use our God-given authority for their benefit. We may need to resist negative thoughts or structures, but that should not be our major preoccupation. As a doctor my focus is helping people to live as full a life as possible. In order to do that, I might have to help them overcome sickness, but my focus is on health not sickness.

In the same way Christians are meant to use their authority to enrich life just as Jesus did. Let's look at some of the ways in which He did it.

It is time to take up our God-given authority and use it wisely.

## Unwrapping the Bonds

Can you recognize within yourself the use of authority in different ways?

Are you tempted to use any authority you have as a means of self-promotion?

How can you use your authority more effectively for the benefit of others?

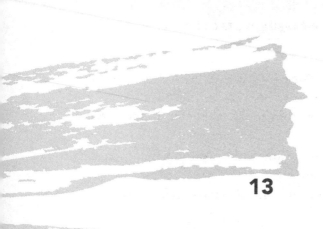

# 13

# UNWRAPPING JESUS' AUTHORITY

## *Revealing the Ability to Serve Others*

My relationship to power and authority is that I'm all for it. People need somebody to watch over them. Ninety-five percent of the people in the world need to be told what to do and how to behave.

Arnold Schwarzenegger

Anyone who conducts an argument by appealing to authority is not using his intelligence; he is just using his memory.

Leonardo da Vinci

These two quotes indicate differing philosophies about authority and leadership. On the one side is the idea that most people need help in knowing what to do or how to behave—and in that context we might be thankful that there are people with the gift of leadership who can make important decisions that benefit others. On the other side is the idea that everyone should be trained how to think and enter into meaningful discussions and deliberations for himself.

The subject of authority is one that has caused me to search the Bible more than any other topic over the last year or so. As I wrote in the last chapter, my model for the use of authority is heavily influenced by my career in medicine, and this has affected my style of leadership. I believe, as both a physician and a minister of the Gospel, that I have been given authority for other people's benefit; this is different from having authority over people.

Let's have a look at some Bible passages that can shed light on this issue of authority.

## The Basis of Our Authority

This first passage has become important in my thinking about the question of authority because it indicates that there are different sources and levels of authority. When the chief priests and the elders question Jesus' authority, He asks them a question in return.

> Jesus entered the temple courts, and, while he was teaching, the chief priests and the elders of the people came to him. "By what authority are you doing these things?" they asked. "And who gave you this authority?"
>
> Jesus replied, "I will also ask you one question. If you answer me, I will tell you by what authority I am doing these things. John's baptism—where did it come from? Was it from heaven, or from men?"

147

They discussed it among themselves and said, "If we say, 'From heaven,' he will ask, 'Then why didn't you believe him?' But if we say, 'From men'—we are afraid of the people, for they all hold that John was a prophet.'"

So they answered Jesus, "We don't know."

Then he said, "Neither will I tell you by what authority I am doing these things."

Matthew 21:23–27

In this passage Jesus, the priests, the elders and the general Jewish populace all understand the difference between God's authority and man's authority.

The religious leaders, rather than disputing these two different sources, work through the consequences of giving either one as an answer to Jesus' question. Authority from heaven carries more weight and importance than authority from a human source. Yet if they acknowledge that John had a heavenly calling, they risk pronouncing themselves hypocrites for not listening to him. If, on the other hand, they reply that John's baptism was from men, they would be denying that John was indeed a prophet, as the people held him to be.

The point I want to make is that no one in the story questions differing sources of authority. I believe that receiving authority from heaven and using it correctly results in the release of the resources of heaven. Alternatively, human authority can release only human resources—and if we have only human resources available to us, we have to rely on human effort to try and fulfill our callings.

Galatians 3:1 has something strong to say about this idea of human effort vs. authority from heaven: "You foolish Galatians! Who has bewitched you? Before your very eyes Jesus Christ was clearly portrayed as crucified."

Paul calls the Galatians foolish. Even stronger than that, he asks who has "bewitched" them, or placed them under a spell in order to control them. This is a serious issue: It strikes at the root of freedom that is at the heart of the Christian Gospel. Look at the next verse: "I would like to learn just one thing from you: Did you receive the Spirit by observing the law, or by believing what you heard?" (Galatians 3:2).

One question can settle the matter, he says. It involves the way in which they received the Holy Spirit: Was it by grace or by human works?

Where the Spirit of the Lord is, there is freedom. Alternatively, trying to receive the Holy Spirit on the basis of our own effort and works is a route that, in terms of our use of authority, will lead toward manipulation and control. "Are you so foolish? After beginning with the Spirit, are you now trying to attain your goal by human effort?" (Galatians 3:3).

Paul is saying this: We were not born again by our own effort. We started our adventure of faith by the grace of God. It makes no sense to try to complete it through our own resources.

"Have you suffered so much for nothing—if it really was for nothing?" he asks. "Does God give you his Spirit and work miracles among you because you observe the law, or because you believe what you heard?" (Galatians 3:4–5). Receiving the Holy Spirit and working miracles are linked. We cannot produce miracles by our own effort, no matter how hard we work. We are completely dependent upon God to work miracles because the authority that initiates them is from heaven not from earth.

Human works can produce some impressive things—large churches, social programs, amazing music. But only through the activity of the Holy Spirit can we produce heavenly things. Without the Holy Spirit we do not have true Christianity because we do not have God at work in us.

Miracles are an essential part of Christianity. They are a demonstration of heaven on earth and can be released only by heaven's authority given to us.

Acts 14:3 states that "Paul and Barnabas spent considerable time there, speaking boldly for the Lord, who confirmed the message of his grace by enabling them to do miraculous signs and wonders."

The message of grace, which is the heart of the Christian Gospel, is confirmed by miraculous signs and wonders. Only God can enable us to do miracles by giving us authority from heaven. Man's authority cannot release miracles, and without them the Christian message lacks the fullness of confirmation that is available.

## Rightly Using Our Heavenly Authority

Please allow me to ask a slightly provocative question.

If you were to start a new church, how would you do it?

Would you seek to gather enough people together to build a sustainable community, with sufficient human resources in order to maintain good meetings that will attract other people—with good music, children's work, preaching—hoping to gather even more people so that the church would grow and become even more effective?

At North Kent Community Church we have done this on a couple of occasions, successfully planting two new churches that have grown and become good churches in their own right. We know this model and have been relatively successful with it.

I am not sure, however, that we would follow this model again. Why not? Because it is mainly dependent upon the gathering of human resources and not upon heaven's resources. It does not depend upon miracles to confirm our message and attract people to God. Rather it seeks to attract people to us, in order to then convey the Christian message.

I am not saying this has been, or is, wrong. I am simply stating that anything founded on human effort carries the danger of leading us away from the Holy Spirit.

This is true for any area of Kingdom living. Whether we are feeding the homeless, serving on the church's leadership team, teaching Sunday school or supporting missionaries, I believe we need to remember the principle of "seeking first the Kingdom." Demonstrating the Kingdom of heaven by using heaven's authority to release heaven's resources on earth will attract people to God—people who can then be born again, baptized and joined together into God's family.

Look, for example, at Acts 8. Here is the story of Philip going to Samaria as a result of the persecution in Jerusalem.

> Those who had been scattered preached the word wherever they went. Philip went down to a city in Samaria and proclaimed the Christ there. When the crowds heard Philip and saw the miraculous signs he did, they all paid close attention to what he said. With shrieks, evil spirits came out of many, and many paralytics and cripples were healed. So there was great joy in that city.
>
> Acts 8:4–8

What do we know about Philip? Not much except that he was a man full of the Holy Spirit and wisdom (see Acts 6:5).

What did he do when he got to Samaria? He proclaimed the Christ there.

How did he do it? He spoke and he performed miracles. The outcome of the miracles was that the crowd paid close attention to what he said. The ultimate outcome was that there was great joy in the city of Samaria. This all came about through heaven's authority and resources being released on earth through one man.

When the apostles in Jerusalem heard about what was happening in Samaria they sent Peter and John there.

When they arrived, they prayed for them that they might receive the Holy Spirit, because the Holy Spirit had not yet come upon any of them; they had simply been baptized into the name of the Lord Jesus. Then Peter and John placed their hands on them, and they received the Holy Spirit.

Acts 8:15–17

What was the priority for Peter and John? To ensure that each believer was filled with the Holy Spirit.

Why is this so important? To ensure that having been born again by the Spirit, people live their Christian lives by the Spirit, enjoying intimacy with God and releasing heaven's resources in their everyday experience. This is the essence of Christianity, and it is based on the amazing grace of God.

The church in Samaria was birthed through the activity of the Holy Spirit and the aim of the apostles was that it would continue in the same way.

So how should heavenly authority be used?

As the time approached for him to be taken up to heaven, Jesus resolutely set out for Jerusalem. And he sent messengers on ahead, who went into a Samaritan village to get things ready for him; but the people there did not welcome him, because he was heading for Jerusalem. When the disciples James and John saw this, they asked, "Lord, do you want us to call fire down from heaven to destroy them?" But Jesus turned and rebuked them, and they went to another village.

Luke 9:51–56

As we look at this Bible passage we find that James and John are confident that they have authority from heaven. When Jesus answers them He does not question or dispute the fact that they *could* call down fire from heaven in the same manner that Elijah had done. The issue is how they should use such authority.

Jesus rebuked them for their thinking and motivation. Their minds were still centered on the old covenant, but Jesus was introducing a new covenant in which the judgment and wrath of God would be satisfied by His sacrifice on the cross. His resurrection to new life and His ascension would release the resources of heaven. In this new covenant, authority should be used to save people rather than destroy them; to save people from sin, sickness, torment, anxiety; to produce freedom rather than slavery and control.

## Jesus' Teaching

In Matthew 20 we find another story that helps us to understand how to be like Jesus in our use of authority:

> Then the mother of Zebedee's sons came to Jesus with her sons and, kneeling down, asked a favor of him.
>
> "What is it you want?" he asked.
>
> She said, "Grant that one of these two sons of mine may sit at your right and the other at your left in your kingdom."
>
> "You don't know what you are asking," Jesus said to them. "Can you drink the cup I am going to drink?"
>
> "We can," they answered.
>
> Jesus said to them, "You will indeed drink from my cup, but to sit at my right or left is not for me to grant. These places belong to those for whom they have been prepared by my Father."
>
> When the ten heard about this, they were indignant with the two brothers. Jesus called them together and said, "You know that the rulers of the Gentiles lord it over them, and their high officials exercise authority over them. Not so with you. Instead, whoever wants to become great among you must be your servant, and whoever wants to be first must be your slave—just as the

Son of Man did not come to be served, but to serve, and to give his life as a ransom for many."

Matthew 20:20–28

This mother of James and John comes to Jesus to ask for something, ambition burning within for her two sons. She wants Jesus to use His authority to give them position and prominence.

When the rest of the disciples hear about this they become indignant. We are not told exactly why, but I think from Jesus' response we can work out that they, too, had some selfish ambition within them for prominence and position.

Jesus points out how earthly rulers use their authority in a way that places them above other people in order to try to exercise authority over them.

"Not so with you," says Jesus.

He is pointing to a different way of doing things. He is showing us the way that authority from heaven *should* be used. Authority from heaven is given in order to serve others, not gain position over them. God has given us authority over sickness, for example, so that people can be set free, not to make us look or feel more important. Likewise, we have been given authority over demons so that we can set people free to be all that God has made them to be, serving their destiny. This should be done unconditionally without strings attached.

I am amazed constantly by the way that Jesus served people unconditionally, requiring nothing from them in return. True, He would give an invitation to follow Him, but He never demanded that people follow Him. Even the twelve disciples are given the choice to follow or not.

Heaven's authority is meant to be dispensed with grace—unconditional love and favor given to others. When authority is used in a way that restricts freedom, we have reason to question where it is coming from.

As I said previously, earthly authority is necessary within society. Institutions such as policing, taxation, the operation of the armed forces, etc. are necessary in order to maintain a stable society. When Christians adopt the same model, however, hoping to release the resources of heaven, it is not likely to work. Heavenly authority needs to be used in accordance with heaven's principles to release heaven's resources.

John 17 helps us understand further:

> After Jesus said this, he looked toward heaven and prayed: "Father, the time has come. Glorify your Son, that your Son may glorify you. For you granted him authority over all people that he might give eternal life to all those you have given him. Now this is eternal life: that they may know you, the only true God, and Jesus Christ, whom you have sent."
>
> John 17:1–3

This passage is the only place I have found in the New Testament that talks about Jesus having authority over people. Elsewhere, it seems to me, the example of Jesus' authority is used for people, not over them. So what is this passage saying?

Jesus has authority over all people. He is God, so this should come as no surprise!

What is the purpose of this authority? To give eternal life.

The purpose of godly authority is to give life. Not just a bit of life, but eternal life. And this is eternal life—to know God.

When Jesus is asked about His authority to forgive sins, He uses His authority over sickness to validate His claim. When we use the authority God has given us to heal the sick, set people free, multiply food, speak directly to people's hearts, perform miracles such as stopping storms and so on, then we give people an opportunity to know this God, to know forgiveness of sin and to enter into eternal life.

Conversely, when we use a different form of authority and attach God's name to it, we give people a false impression of God that may hinder them from truly knowing Him. A good example occurred during the Middle Ages at the time of the Inquisition. The Church used its authority to rule over people through fear and guilt. It is no surprise then that people viewed God in the same way, perceiving that He was harsh and cruel. They could only relate to Him through guilt and fear.

Unfortunately, some of those principles were not left behind in the Middle Ages. It is too common to see people weighed down with guilt and fear when it comes to relating to God. This happens because they are being asked to submit to people who exercise human (as opposed to heavenly) authority over them in the name of Christian leadership rather than help them find the freedom, peace, joy, righteousness and other fruit of the Gospel of the Kingdom.

## A Different Way of Doing Things

The way we use authority within Christianity is vitally important because it has a profound effect on the way that people perceive God. In Matthew 8 we find the story of the centurion's servant:

> When Jesus had entered Capernaum, a centurion came to him, asking for help. "Lord," he said, "my servant lies at home paralyzed and in terrible suffering."
>
> Jesus said to him, "I will go and heal him."
>
> The centurion replied, "Lord, I do not deserve to have you come under my roof. But just say the word, and my servant will be healed. For I myself am a man under authority, with soldiers under me. I tell this one, 'Go,' and he goes; and that one, 'Come,' and he comes. I say to my servant, 'Do this,' and he does it."

When Jesus heard this, he was astonished and said to those following him, "I tell you the truth, I have not found anyone in Israel with such great faith. I say to you that many will come from the east and the west, and will take their places at the feast with Abraham, Isaac and Jacob in the kingdom of heaven. But the subjects of the kingdom will be thrown outside, into the darkness, where there will be weeping and gnashing of teeth."

Then Jesus said to the centurion, "Go! It will be done just as you believed it would." And his servant was healed at that very hour.

Matthew 8:5–13

In this story we get further insight into authority. The correct understanding of authority will build our faith. If we understand how God's authority works, we will have great faith to use it in amazing ways.

In this instance, the centurion understands that Jesus has authority over sickness: He simply needs to say the word and sickness has to leave. This soldier is helped in his understanding by his military background. He knows that he has authority over other men. If he says, "Go," they will go.

Please note, this is an example of how authority works generally and the centurion is illustrating it from his own life. It is not a template for Christian leadership.

Jesus gives us the better example: He exercises authority over the sickness and it goes. This is a model for healing.

Simply because the centurion uses his earthly model to explain his understanding of Jesus' heavenly authority over sickness and demons, it would be wrong, in my opinion, to think this justifies the idea of Christian leaders exercising authority over other people.

I have often heard this passage used to address the question, Whose authority are you under? The implication is that this story serves as a model for church structures, affirming a hierarchy of human leadership. I believe this is contrary to the broader teaching of the Bible, specifically the passage in Matthew 20 regarding the mother's request for her two sons. It is also an inappropriate use of this passage in Matthew 8.

This leads us to another vital question: What about *submission?*

Submission is part of biblical teaching. Indeed the book of James tells us that the wisdom that comes down from heaven is submissive. So we need to marry up heavenly authority with heavenly submission, and we will need heavenly wisdom to do so!

Within Christianity I have all too often seen the call for people to submit to leadership structures that have been based on earthly authority and wisdom. Structures that do not require the miraculous, supernatural working of the Holy Spirit will inevitably be based on the human resources available. Submission in this context is usually along designated lines of human authority, with some people placed in positions of authority over others.

I believe that the Bible teaches us to submit to one another in accordance to the measure of heavenly authority and gifting that has been given by God to individuals and churches. I choose to submit myself to other people in whom I recognize certain spiritual gifts from God, because I want to learn from them and receive heaven's resources through them.

Those same people can choose to submit to me, if they wish, in the areas where God has gifted me, so that they receive the resources I have available.

We can submit to each other in a loving, non-hierarchical way, receiving from one another the heavenly resources that God has placed within us. In this way we can be the Body of Christ joined together in the way that the Holy Spirit has designed.

Within this context the Holy Spirit will give the gift of leadership (as taught in Romans 13) to which others can submit. This leadership is not given in order to rule over others, but rather to serve others by creating an environment of grace, love, joy, peace and freedom within which people can truly know and experience God in increasing measure and enjoy each other in a mutually supportive way.

Mutual love and submission will create an environment in which Jesus' authority can be released in increasing measure. In this safety, we find that we all have an equally important part in making God known to others in increasing measure.

It is time to throw off the restraints of Christian structures built on human authority and release the goodness and power of God through the exercise of godly authority in a godly manner.

## Unwrapping the Bonds

What resources are you drawing upon for authority within the Body of Christ—man's or God's?

Do you agree that authority and submission should walk hand in hand? How might this look in your own walk of faith?

How do you distinguish human authority from heavenly authority?

What is an example of an appropriate use of each in your life?

# 14

# UNWRAPPING ANGELS
## Revealing These Servants of Heaven

His name is Gold. He is an angel.

More about him later.

A few years ago, when the subject of angels became highlighted for me, I realized that in almost twenty years of leading a church and working with other churches, I had never taught about angels. Actually, I could not remember ever hearing a sermon about angels. I had received and given plenty of instruction about demons and how to combat them, but never about these servants of heaven we call angels.

So once again I set off on a Bible study.

The Bible has many references to angels. It is difficult to find significant advances in God's purposes in the New Testament that are not announced by angels or that do not include their involvement in some way (the Day of Pentecost and Paul's conversion are a couple of exceptions).

Here are some examples:

- The conception of Jesus in Mary
- Joseph's revelation about Mary and his responsibility to protect her
- The birth of Jesus
- Jesus in the wilderness after His temptation
- Jesus in the Garden of Gethsemane
- The empty tomb
- Jesus' ascension into heaven
- Peter's release from prison
- The story of Cornelius and the breakthrough of the Gospel into the Gentile world
- The letters in chapters 2–3 of the book of Revelation are written to the angel of each church (I am still working on understanding that!)

Somehow I had missed this important aspect of the Bible, acknowledging the existence of angels without acknowledging their importance.

So having done the study I started to do some teaching—and I was surprised by the response I got. Many people asked why they had never heard this before and were delighted to discover another aspect of Christianity. Others started to accuse our church of having a preoccupation with angels. A rumor was sent round in some Christian circles that we had started to worship angels in our church—wholly untrue, may I add.

I had to ask myself why the negative responses were coming.

The greatest negative reaction to our church's teaching involved the idea that angels have names, and that we might interact with them while knowing and using their names. This reaction was perplexing to me because the Bible clearly speaks of angels by their names. Granted, most references to angels in the Bible do not include their names, but the same is true of many humans: the woman with the hemorrhage, the centurion, the ten lepers, among many others.

The reaction seemed out of proportion and not in line with biblical thinking. When I detect such things it usually indicates that the issue has spiritual importance. I have learned in these instances to pay special attention to what Holy Spirit is saying, to what the Bible teaches and to the opinions of people around me whom I respect.

So why is this an important issue to unwrap?

I believe it is important because it reveals another aspect of relying upon the spiritual realm and not just our earthly realm. The concept of angels at work among us challenges those who rely primarily on human, earthly authority rather than heavenly authority. It is another aspect of heaven invading earth.

In addition, angels are opposed by demons, so it is an important aspect of spiritual warfare. In Daniel 10–12 we are given insight into spiritual warfare in the spiritual realm. We see that God sends angels in response to our prayers (just as an angel was sent in response to Cornelius' prayers in the book of Acts) and that they have to battle with demons to bring those answers. Daniel 12:1 talks about Michael, who protects the people of God. Protection sounds good!

I came to the conclusion that this is an important issue for Christians and an aspect of God's provision for and goodness to us—an important heavenly resource. After all, if Jesus needed help from angels, who am I to think that I do not?

## An Unseen Resource

A story from the book of 2 Kings should help us. We find it in chapter 6:

Now the king of Aram was at war with Israel. After conferring with his officers, he said, "I will set up my camp in such and such a place."

The man of God sent word to the king of Israel: "Beware of passing that place, because the Arameans are going down there." So the king of Israel checked on the place indicated by the man of God. Time and again Elisha warned the king, so that he was on his guard in such places.

This enraged the king of Aram. He summoned his officers and demanded of them, "Will you not tell me which of us is on the side of the king of Israel?"

"None of us, my lord the king," said one of his officers, "but Elisha, the prophet who is in Israel, tells the king of Israel the very words you speak in your bedroom."

"Go, find out where he is," the king ordered, "so I can send men and capture him." The report came back: "He is in Dothan." Then he sent horses and chariots and a strong force there. They went by night and surrounded the city.

When the servant of the man of God got up and went out early the next morning, an army with horses and chariots had surrounded the city. "Oh, my lord, what shall we do?" the servant asked.

"Don't be afraid," the prophet answered. "Those who are with us are more than those who are with them."

And Elisha prayed, "O LORD, open his eyes so he may see." Then the LORD opened the servant's eyes, and he looked and saw the hills full of horses and chariots of fire all around Elisha.

2 Kings 6:8–17

In the context of warfare, God enables Elisha to know the enemy's movements and warn the king of Israel beforehand, so that he can be on guard. When the king of Aram learns about this, he endeavors to capture Elisha. His troops surround the city of Dothan. When Elisha's servant wakes up and sees the enemy force surrounding them, immediately fear grips him. He has no idea what to do—except talk to Elisha. Elisha sees the man's fear and tells him not to be afraid.

Let's pause here in the story. Given the circumstances, it is quite reasonable for the servant to be afraid. They are in grave danger. The servant, however, is not seeing the full picture. He is looking only with human eyes. He has no idea of the angelic resources of heaven that have already been released for them.

Elisha has a much fuller perspective. I think it is fair to presume that he is enjoying the peace of God. He states to his servant, "Those who are with us are more than those who are with them."

Simple human calculation would seem to contradict this statement. In terms of human resources, they are outnumbered! It would be reasonable, from a purely human point of view, to think Elisha is either misguided, detached from reality, untruthful or overly optimistic. His servant could contest his statement and its conclusion. He could also question Elijah's demeanor: "Why aren't you afraid? At least try to do something rather than just rest there!"

Elisha prays and suddenly the servant sees the bigger picture. Immediately his fear is transformed into faith as he sees the resources of heaven deployed for them.

I have seen something similar to this scene played out many times when people tell me about their adverse circumstances, often with a degree of anxiety in their voices. Humanly speaking, things look bleak. I sense that they expect me to join in their anxiety as an appropriate response to what is happening.

Rather than embrace a view that is dictated by limited human resources, however, I try to help people open their eyes to the greater reality of heaven's resources available to them. I like to take them on the journey out of fear into faith as God reveals His goodness to them. If all we can see are human resources, then we will struggle to overcome the flaming darts of fear and anxiety that the devil will throw at us. Seeing heaven's resources can increase our faith and confidence in God.

The ability to see the resources of heaven can be astonishing and life-transforming. Some people have the ability to see into this realm all the time, but the majority of us need to use our "eyes of faith" to see into this unseen realm; sometimes (and I hope increasingly) we can see signs of such things with our own physical eyes.

I believe, for example, that the current phenomenon of gold dust/particles and feathers appearing among us is one such sign. These phenomena direct us to look more closely with our eyes of faith and encourage us in our faith. (There are many references in the Bible to wings as a sign of God's activity, and gold is linked to God's glory.)

Whichever way it is for you, I believe that God wants to open our eyes to see more. In order for this to happen, we need to be faithful with the little things that God places in front of us.

How do you respond to manifestations like gold dust and feathers?

How do you respond to stories of angels among us?

When you hear stories of miracles, does your heart overflow with thankfulness or is it overwhelmed by a mind full of questions?

I have learned to rejoice at the mysteries of God and the signs of His activity—trying to notice when His gentle voice is attempting to get my attention. I regularly see gold dust on people's faces in meetings, in public, during meals, and I rejoice over each occasion. I do not seek such signs, but I take notice.

Recently, while visiting a cathedral in Spain, I was standing in the large main sanctuary within the enormous structure, wondering at the splendor and beauty of it all. I had just noticed a side chapel dedicated to the Holy Spirit, which is unusual to my recollection. As I was standing in the sanctuary, talking with God, a feather slowly fell to the floor by my side. I looked up to see where it might have come from. There was no obvious source. I picked it up from the floor and marveled once again that God was interacting with me in such a way. What was He saying? I am still meditating on that.

The feather is in a small plastic bag in my wallet, alongside another one that "appeared" in our house and also a small stone that God gave to me in an unusual way. I keep them with me as reminders and signs. I have chosen to value them as a sign of heaven's resources made available to me. In terms of human resources they mean next to nothing, but upon me they make a huge impact.

A good prayer as we push further into this subject is, "Lord, open my eyes that I may see."

My suggestion is that, having prayed, we then value the things we begin to see.

And so back to Gold.

## Having Eyes to See

I have recounted how, in April 2009, Kim and I left our house in the U.K. and set off for a three-month adventure in California at Bethel Church, Redding. We threw ourselves into the life of the church in every way we could.

Two weeks later I traveled to Wisconsin with my friend Chris Gore, who was speaking at a healing conference. I had the privilege of also being involved. I had a great time. My most prominent memory is seeing the face of a woman—about forty years old and profoundly deaf since birth—as she realized that she could hear.

Meanwhile, back in Redding, Kim was attending some

meetings of the School of Supernatural Ministry. I will let Kim's own words tell the story.

After two weeks in Redding, Pete left town for four days and I had the privilege of being able to attend the School of Supernatural Ministry at Bethel. James Maloney was a guest speaker, and he shared his testimony, which was like no other I had ever heard. I heard things that blew my mind and my theology! After his talk he explained that he would be praying a prayer of impartation. Having just heard amazing, faith-stirring and faith-challenging things, I stood with hundreds of others as he prayed.

Standing quietly with my hands slightly raised, all I can say is that out of my "spiritual peripheral vision" I became aware, on my right, of a large angelic being. He was big and gold and muscular. I stood there, glancing to my right, thinking, *What do you do when you are aware of an angel? This has never happened to me before!*

Then a phrase came into my mind (I now think that the reason God put it in my mind in this form was so that I would know it was not from me, since it did not fit my theology at all). The phrase was: *I have an angel and his name is Gold.* I had no idea what to do with this. Then two words came clearly into my head: *gold* and *sword.* As I waited, I saw a large, gold flaming sword. I had the sense that I was to hold the sword with an up-stretched arm, and that as I did so, something would happen in the heavenlies that would enable people to stream past into freedom and liberty. Still standing quietly, I tried to evaluate what was happening. It was all a bit too big for me! I was still aware of the angel and of the presence of God. Was this really happening or was I on an ego trip? It felt a bit like a commissioning.

Pete and I work with a group of churches in France, and we have visited the beaches in Normandy where Allied forces landed on D-Day. The Holy Spirit reminded me that the code names for two of those beaches were "Gold" and "Sword." In the days following D-Day, two temporary harbors were built, one on Omaha Beach and one on Gold Beach. Two weeks after D-Day, however, a storm damaged both harbors. The harbor on Omaha Beach was put permanently out of action. The harbor on Gold Beach was repaired, and men and resources needed for the liberation poured through this beachhead for the next ten months.

I had the sense that God was saying, *You have a beachhead anointing. As you establish something and hold ground in the heavenly realms, this will enable people to come into the freedom and liberation that is in My heart for them.*

I stood feeling overwhelmed. It felt like a holy moment . . . so big. God was saying amazing things, but it was only between me and Him. What weight could I give to what I had just experienced? Later that day I emailed Pete: "I've got something to share with you when you get back."

Four days later I picked up Pete from the airport, and we drove straight to the Leaders Advance Conference for the next three days. On the last day, a woman from Texas, whom we had never met, asked if she could prophesy over us. I will let Pete take up the story from here.

Kim was confronted by an experience that went beyond her previous experience. She had a choice to make: She could either trust God with what He was revealing to her and also trust the environment, the church, in which this was taking place or not. She allowed "childlike faith" to triumph over questions and even doubts, and she pressed into what God was doing and saying. She inclined her ear to God. She used her mind to gain further insight through previous knowledge and experience. She was suddenly more aware of heaven's authority and resources, and her own calling and destiny. With faith and courage she embraced what God was doing and saying, and that moment quite literally became a gateway into our future destiny with God.

On the last day of the conference the woman Kim mentioned, Mignon Murrell, prophesied over us. It was a prophecy of vast proportions and difficult to take in all in one go, so I asked if she could write it down and send it to us. This she did, obviously praying some more and hearing more from God for us.

Here are some extracts from what she sent to us:

The Lord showed me that He has chosen you guys to make history in the U.K. (again, I don't normally give people words like this unless the Lord says they are ready to receive it). You are revivalists whose story is going to be recorded for history's sake. He showed me that you had warriors, military people, in your generational lines. This is actually an anointing for victorious warfare and strategy that He has released over your line, which will be helpful to you in battling and receiving divine strategies of battle against the principalities and rulers over your region.

The Lord also said that He is giving you increased favor and influence with important government people in your country. He is granting you greater influence with these people because of your heart—your heart for God is what is moving the Lord to grant this increasing influence. He also showed me that you have a heart for the youth or rather the next generation (this is more than just youth), and He has called you to help and have influence over the next generation in the U.K. You will have a significant impact on their lives!

I also saw that you are getting a new angelic guard to help you in this task. (I see into the spirit and see angels all of the time.) I saw a very large angel standing over you that was wearing/holding a coat of arms. I have never seen this before, but I noticed that on the coat of arms was a lion that appeared to have wings. This is significant for your task and speaks of the role this angel will play in helping you with your task. Again, I feel that it has to do with your influence in government, but I encourage you to give this to your intercessors and see what the Lord reveals to them about it. I did not get the angel's full name, but think it started with G.

I *do* think you will encounter this angel in the future and will be given more understanding about it. As a pastor, you already know the importance of God's government in the Kingdom. I believe that in the coming season, the Lord is going to reveal to you more of how His government in heaven works, so you can see a true Kingdom model and gain greater understanding so you can implement that in your sphere of influence.

Another thing I saw was that the Holy Spirit is going to take you into a time of experiencing a fuller measure of His presence. I saw what looked like a Holy Spirit "takeover" of your life in many different areas. Not that you aren't already sensitive to His presence—you are—this is more like a serious upgrade and greater infilling. While praying for you on Wednesday night I saw that your ministry was going to be like a sword thrust into the U.K. and that when this sword went into the ground it was a demarcation, a battle line in the spirit, and caused an earthquake in the surrounding region.

I also saw that Kim is going to be given a ministry of joy that brings the miraculous.

As you can imagine, such a prophecy was not easy to comprehend. Who were we to receive such thoughts? It would have been easy to dismiss or play down the significance. But God had prepared us by revealing an angel called Gold to Kim. The reference in Mignon's prophecy to an angel whose name starts with the letter G was an astounding confirmation, and then the reference to a sword as well.

Truly our eyes had been opened in greater measure.

## Which View Will We Take?

The story of Gideon comes to mind here.

God called him a mighty warrior when he was hiding from his enemy and his estimation of himself was extremely low.

God had a different perspective, which He chose to reveal. Understanding God's perspective and embracing it is vital if we are to understand and fulfill our destinies.

Take Mary for example. While not understanding in human terms, she embraced the will of God for her life, carried the Son of God in her womb and gave birth to the Savior of the world. How did God reveal His plan to her? By sending an angel. This fundamental act is welcomed by Christians and celebrated by much of the world each Christmas. Why is it so hard to believe that God would continue to use His angels as messengers and helpers?

The challenge for Kim and me was whether we would embrace God's view of ourselves or limit ourselves to our own human perspective. False humility rose its head at that time and gave us an attitude that was inclined to dismiss such grand thoughts. Even today, writing this chapter, I find myself hesitant to include the prophecy—probably due to thoughts about how people might react to it. Fear, pride and false humility will attack us to try and keep us back from attempting and doing great exploits for God.

Denying the thoughts of God toward us is not true humility; it is actually pride, placing our thoughts above those of God. True humility will embrace God's perspective with the understanding that only God's resources are sufficient to enable us to fulfill His purposes.

Such thinking will help us develop our relationship with Holy Spirit and keep us reliant upon God. Instead of pride it will give us greater opportunity to live in true humility, just as Jesus did when He walked upon the earth. Embracing the revelations God wishes to bring to us will lead us into greater adventures of faith.

Within ten days of returning from California, Kim and I were in France to lead a Bible camp. We were praying and worshiping together with the leadership team at the beginning of the week.

At the end of this time, a close friend of ours, Julian Adams, came up to Kim (with no knowledge of our recent experience) and asked if she had had any angelic encounters while in Redding, because all during the worship and prayer time he had seen a gold warrior angel standing behind her!

At the beginning of September that year a man visited our church for the first time, at its normal Sunday venue. Later in conversation, he told me he had seen a large gold angel standing at the entrance as he arrived. God told him that this angel had been assigned to our church to help us with our mission.

About a year later I was speaking at a healing conference. As I got up onto the platform to speak, a woman gasped loudly. At the end of that session she told me that as I took the podium, a large gold angel walked through the wall to stand behind me all the time I was speaking.

As you can imagine, these happenings have served to encourage, strengthen and comfort us. They have helped us to take seriously God's prophetic words to us and pursue them passionately and confidently, knowing that He is with us.

Part of the outworking of all this is that we have established a School of Supernatural Ministry based at North Kent Community Church. God has clearly called us to do this. We had initially developed an evening school and then He told us to start our daytime school and begin in September 2010. In April 2010 we had no money for this project, no premises and no students. The temptation to stop was obvious, but faith kept us going because we had heard the word of God and He had revealed His help for us. We started, and the school has flourished and become an amazing environment in which people can encounter God and grow in faith.

I am aware that this chapter could provoke all sorts of thoughts and questions. In the next chapter I will try to explain from the Bible how we can receive more of God's heavenly resources for us. May I encourage you to pray that God will open your eyes to see more of the angelic reality?

It is time to throw off the false humility that would restrict us to human resources and human thinking, so that we can embrace God's perspective and see more clearly.

## Unwrapping the Bonds

In matters of spiritual warfare, do you generally feel like Elisha or his unseeing servant?

Do you think that God ever sends angels to help you?

Are you willing to ask God to reveal them to you? Why or why not?

# 15

# UNWRAPPING MALNOURISHMENT

## Revealing Hindrances to Spiritual Health

A number of years ago one of my patients came to see me about losing weight. She was very overweight, probably weighing in at nearly three times her optimal size. She was a jovial person, and I used to enjoy seeing her and chatting. Despite my best attempts to help her, however, she never managed to sustain any substantial loss of weight. Health problems loomed on the horizon.

Then it happened! The pounds started to drop off her. She was happy, I was happy, everyone was happy. She did not know how she was doing it, but things were definitely changing.

The weight continued to fall off, and she started to fit into nice dresses that made her feel good about herself. Such a transformation! Everyone was amazed.

My mind, however, was processing what was going on. This was an unexplained loss of weight to a degree that was highly unusual. I grew concerned.

I went away on vacation, and on my return she came to see me. While I had been away, she had begun to feel unwell, had consulted one of my colleagues and had agreed to undergo an investigation. The possibility of cancer raised its head. Numerous tests took place, all of which revealed nothing to help us. By this time she had started to feel very ill. Everyone prepared for the worst.

Then a thought came into my head: *malabsorption*. There are various medical conditions that can cause weight loss. One of these is malabsorption. This is when food taken into the body does not get digested and absorbed properly. The nutrients do not all enter into the bloodstream. One of the causes of this can be celiac disease. I arranged for a diagnostic test to be done, and it came back positive.

The treatment for this is a gluten-free diet. Once this was put into place, this dear lady started to feel much better and gained weight once again. Instead of looking as though she was at death's door, she began to live life to the full again. Back on went all of the weight she had lost, and we resumed our original conversation!

This woman had continued to eat the same things throughout this whole episode until diagnosed with celiac disease. She had not changed her diet at all. So what had happened? Why had she lost weight?

Malabsorption.

Food was of no benefit to her until we realized the truth of her situation and gave her a solution. Following the solution she was able, once again, to benefit from the food she was taking in and nourish her body (albeit it a little too enthusiastically!).

How many of us suffer from spiritual malabsorption?

How many sermons have we heard?

How many books have we read?

How many podcasts . . . prophecies . . . testimonies . . . conferences?

Not many of us (certainly in developed countries) lack the opportunity for spiritual input.

We should all be spiritual giants. And yet . . .

Spiritual malabsorption is a common malady. So much input, so little growth. How many sermons have I listened to, how many chapters of the Bible read and reread? So much head knowledge. Even when we have grown in faith in the past, has that growth been sustained?

I have mentioned my trips to Mexico, which I have taken on a number of occasions in order to work with churches in different locations—particularly, El Bethi, a small rural farming community. When I asked my friend Leonardo how they had produced such an amazing church family there, he responded, "The little we know, we do."

Christian maturity is not measured by head knowledge, but by our hearts and our willingness to step out in faith according to the measure of revelation we have received.

## Seeing the Consequences

Let's look at a Bible passage to try to help us find a solution to this issue of spiritual malabsorption, so that we can benefit from all the spiritual nutrition available to us. This is a verse that I used to read and consider somewhat unfair. Perhaps you are familiar with it: "Therefore consider carefully how you listen. Whoever has will be given more; whoever does not have, even what he thinks he has will be taken from him" (Luke 8:18).

Those who have get more, and those who do not have lose what they have? Aside from seeming unfair, it also gets confusing. How can we lose something we do not have? Is God saying He will take things away from us? Will the strong get stronger and the weak get weaker?

I realize now that I had been neglecting the first part of this verse. This is not a statement of God's intention; rather, it indicates the consequences of our behavior: "Consider carefully how you listen. . . ."

How deliberate am I in my listening? How am I allowing the things that enter my mind to shape my thinking? I believe this applies to all input into our brains, not just what comes through our ears.

I find it very interesting that the Bible is talking about how we listen, not what we listen to. I believe, also, that it is primarily talking about the "good things" that we listen to. It is not addressing the issue of guarding ourselves from unhelpful input (important as that is).

So how do we process the good stuff? The nourishing stuff?

I preach regularly in North Kent Community Church and other churches, and I usually try to illustrate what I am saying with encouraging stories that build people's faith. Although you cannot judge everything by people's expressions, they will often give you an indication of the impact of what is being said.

The same story can get a completely different response from people in the same audience. One person can listen to a story of healing and be encouraged and grow in faith; another person can listen to the same story and be discouraged, wondering why someone close to him or her did not get healed.

The same can be true of reading the Bible. How carefully are we listening to what the Holy Spirit is saying through the Bible? Are we simply processing it with our own thoughts?

Let's take the example of a testimony about healing. If you incline your ears to belief and faith while listening to the story, then the level of faith you previously had in that area will grow. Alternatively, if you incline your ears to unbelief and doubt, the goodness from the story will not be properly absorbed into your Christian life, and what has been placed before you will be lost. Even more, the level of faith you previously had in this area could possibly diminish. The opportunity is the same, but the outcome is different. Every circumstance gives an opportunity to grow in faith in some way.

The outcome is a consequence of how we listen.

We know how this works in close relationships. When the relationship is good, communication will tend to be interpreted positively. When the relationship is not so good, misunderstandings and negative interpretations of what has been said occur more frequently.

When you are listening, how do questions form in your mind? Do they form from a desire to know more, understand and grow? Or do they form from a desire to prove yourself correct?

One time I was preaching in another country with the help of a translator. It was at the wedding of a friend, a young lady who had been born and raised in England, but who now lived abroad and was marrying a young man from there. I was reasonably familiar with the other language, but not fluent enough for public speaking. I had carefully prepared what I was going to say, seeking to bless and encourage the newly married couple, and help to give them a foundation of grace and love for their marriage.

As I was speaking, I became alarmed at how my words were being translated. Instead of a message of grace, a different message poured out of the translator's mouth. She was listening to what I was saying and interpreting it completely differently. Her hearing was fashioned by her form of religion, and her mindset changed my meaning.

Unfortunately, there was little I could do in that moment in front of a wedding congregation, but later on I talked with a close friend who was there and who is fluent in both languages in order to ascertain if I had been mistaken in my understanding. Once assured that my words had not been translated correctly, I sought out the married couple and asked the wife, who understood English perfectly, to please explain my message to her husband so that they could start their married life with a common understanding.

I wonder how often our preconceived ideas turn God's words to us into a different message—a message we then pass on to others. Certainly, I have been guilty of interpreting the Bible in a way that is inconsistent with the life of Jesus. On a number of occasions I have apologized to my church for teaching them things that were incorrect. I want to keep learning and be open to the fact that my understanding is incomplete. I want to listen carefully to Holy Spirit so that He can lead me into all truth. I want to absorb all the goodness available into my being, so that it becomes a part of me.

Another way of looking at this is by talking about our eyes. What lenses are we looking through? If we look through blue lenses the world will appear blue. Similarly with green, red or yellow. If we look through the lens of pessimism, things will usually look bleak and negative. The lens of fear and insecurity will distort a confident view of the world.

The lenses of our minds have been formed through our attitudes, upbringing and experiences. They can cause us to reject the good things placed in front of us and miss the nourishment within.

A friend of mine told me a true story about himself. He went to preach at another church. Someone greeted him upon arrival and was excited to state that he had seen three angels accompanying my friend into the building. Unfortunately, my friend replied by saying, "I have the Holy Spirit; I don't need angels." I was saddened by this response because he had rejected part of heaven's provision for himself and closed his ears and eyes to an opportunity to grow. What he had been given, he lost.

I am not sure that I would go so far as to say that he totally lost the help the angels were offering—the story regarding the father of John the Baptist comes to mind—but I do believe that he missed an opportunity to grow spiritually and benefit in greater measure from the resources of heaven.

As I have said previously, we need to be open to continuing revelation about the nature of God because He is infinite and eternal. If we stop listening carefully we will be at risk of spiritual malabsorption. We need to remain open to the voice of the Holy Spirit so that He can lead us into all truth and we can continue to grow.

## What Gets in the Way?

What things can keep us from hearing and seeing properly? What factors do we need to pay careful attention to? What can stop us from absorbing into ourselves the nutrients God makes available?

A verse in the book of Hebrews helps us unwrap this.

> Therefore, since we are surrounded by such a great cloud of witnesses, let us throw off everything that hinders and the sin that so easily entangles, and let us run with perseverance the race marked out for us.
>
> Hebrews 12:1

The Bible tells us to throw off such things that hinder us from knowing Him more fully and growing in faith. What are these things? Here are some hindrances to spiritual health. This is not a complete list, but I hope that it is enough to get you thinking.

### A Closed Mind

Most people would hate to think they have closed their minds, but it is true for most of us that preconceived ideas can stop us from embracing new thoughts. This is certainly the case at Nazareth when Jesus returns there (see Mark 6:1–6). The people of Nazareth probably know Jesus better than anyone else because He grew up among them. They know Him as Mary's son, the carpenter, and they know His brothers and sisters. But they do not want to know Him as a miracle worker and an amazing teacher. Not only do they not want to know Him like that, they take offense at Him. This is not the Jesus they knew!

Familiarity can close our minds to new revelation. How true this can be in Christianity!

In early 1994, God poured out the Holy Spirit in a new and fresh way on a small church in Toronto. The spiritual phenomenon, known as the Toronto Blessing, spread rapidly around the world. Many people were touched. There were outbreaks of joy and wonder. Power was released into people's lives and extraordinary transformation happened.

At our church, on four occasions, we hosted teams from the Toronto church that was at the heart of this move of God. We had wonderful times of enjoying the presence and power of God. We received blessing and pursued new things God was doing—but somehow our church missed something important!

God was speaking a message within the context of signs and wonders, and we missed it. It was a message of the Father's heart and love. He was speaking to His Church to transform her from a mentality of servitude to an understanding of being sons and daughters of the King of kings.

It was not until about 2007 that our ears started to pick up what God had been saying for years.

I know of many other churches that initially enjoyed the blessing but then "moved on" from it. Listening through servants' ears, rather than sons' ears, they returned to work, rather than sit at Jesus' feet (as with Martha and Mary). They stopped pursuing the blessing, and some even spoke against those who continued to pursue it. Still others rejected the move of God altogether for various different reasons. I believe they missed out on part of God's wonderful nutrition for the Body.

### A Slave's Mind

When we listen with the mentality of a slave or, put another way, with the mind of a servant, we have our ears tuned to hear instructions. Slaves and servants receive orders from their masters. They do not expect words of intimacy. They do not expect to be invited to sit at the family table and enjoy a family meal. They do not expect to be involved in the decisions of the family business. A servant's ears will miss much of what God is saying.

In John 15:15 Jesus said,

> "I no longer call you servants, because a servant does not know his master's business. Instead, I have called you friends, for everything that I learned from my Father I have made known to you."

Friends listen differently from servants.

Sons listen differently from servants.

We still serve God—the apostle Paul talked about himself as a servant of God—but this is not our primary identity. We are sons, daughters and friends of God who serve Him happily.

### An Orphan's Mind

Jesus said that He would not leave us as orphans (see John 14:18). An orphan mindset is insecure, looking constantly for affirmation but expecting rejection. It is uncertain of provision and security. It has difficulty looking into the future and concentrates on surviving in the now. It tends to have difficulty forming lasting, heartfelt relationships, and can become self-sufficient in a way that is detached from other people.

An orphan's ears will hear things in a way that makes it difficult to take hold of anything positive. Because of insecurity around parental figures, orphans tend to have difficulty trusting leaders and can react strongly against them if they feel they are not being heard or getting their own way. Much has been said about this in other books, so I will not elaborate further. Suffice it to say that people with an orphan mindset will often not absorb the goodness that is offered to them spiritually.

Insecurity is a powerful filter that stops so much goodness from entering into our minds. But there is an amazing solution—the Holy Spirit is a Spirit of adoption, bringing us into the full rights of sons (see Galatians 4:4–7). He will reveal the truth of the Father's heart to us if we open ourselves to His revelation. He can overcome our insecurities and make us secure in our Father's love.

### A Proud Mind

There is a Bible verse that scares me! It is this: "But he gives us more grace. That is why Scripture says: 'God opposes the proud but gives grace to the humble'" (James 4:6).

Imagine God opposing you!

What would make Him do such a thing?

Pride is at the root of much evil. Its own root is independence from God—being your own god through placing your thinking above His—and its fruit is detachment from God. It was introduced to humans by the devil himself, enticing man and woman to become independent of God, just as he had desired to be when he fought to place himself above God. That is why God opposes it. He wants to be in close relationship with us.

Pride is a mindset that subjects everything to our own thoughts rather than God's thoughts. It knows better than anyone else and easily adopts the position of expert.

I enjoy observing people. The desire to be an expert is common in the human mind. Over the years our family has been on many holidays together, discovering and enjoying new places. Most other holiday makers are similarly discovering new things. I find it amusing how often people who have been in a place for just a few days adopt the position of "holiday expert" for any "newcomers." I dare say that I have done the same—and it is good to be helpful to others; I just find it amusing.

Less amusing to me is when people with little knowledge or training adopt the posture of medical experts. Some things I read in newspapers or see on television make me cringe at their inaccuracy and possible danger to health.

It happens in the realms of Christianity as well.

To me, pride is an attitude that has decided it knows best on a certain subject and is unwilling to learn more. It is not to be confused with confidence in one's own abilities—to deny our abilities is false humility and takes glory away from God, who has given us our abilities. But we can always learn more and improve.

I believe that I am a good doctor, and this confidence helps me to treat my patients well. If, however, I had not continued to learn new things over the thirty years since I qualified, I would now be a bad doctor. The willingness to learn is a vital component of life and, I believe, is the essence of true humility.

It is also important not to confuse pride with correct delight in our own and other people's achievements. I celebrate the achievements of my children, friends and others. I celebrate my own achievements as well, giving thanks and praise to God, who has formed me and enabled me to do such things.

False humility, which denies achievement, will rob us of joy and rob God of the glory He is due.

True humility is having sober assessment of your own strengths and weaknesses and the willingness to learn and improve. The willingness to receive correction is central to this. We all make genuine mistakes that need to be corrected. Remember your math homework? Not correcting mistakes early on will lead to more mistakes in the future. This does not mean, of course, that we should rebuke people for making mistakes. Loving correction is the right response. And willingness to listen is vital in order to learn.

A rebuke should come only in response to sin and rebellion. If we confuse it with correction, and use it when people make genuine mistakes, we will cause fear, hinder learning and stop people from taking the risks from which new discoveries are made.

Proud ears have difficulty hearing new things.

Ears of false humility will miss the celebration of good things.

Humble ears will learn and celebrate.

### A Legalistic Mind

Legalism is a mindset and philosophy that thinks our good deeds can bring us into a better relationship with God and gain His approval and promotion. It is the root of religion. It is denial of the grace of God and the Christian Gospel itself. We will look at this in greater detail in the next chapter, focusing particularly on the book of Galatians.

Legalistic ears do not hear the grace of God and all the goodness contained within it. This is probably one of the biggest spiritual battles the Church has faced through the centuries—the battle for grace. A revelation of the grace of God will open our ears to so much more of His goodness.

### A Cynical Mind

We mentioned a negative, cynical attitude in chapter 11. In some ways this is similar to a proud mind, but it is slightly different. Not necessarily thinking it knows best, this mindset considers its own opinion to be at least the most reliable. Thus, it tends to doubt the validity of other people's thinking. Not only that, it questions and judges other people's motives. It knocks people down rather than build them up. It is slow to rejoice and celebrate, tending to look for the "other side of the story" and identify any inconsistencies or possible flaws.

It tends to think of itself as being more "realistic" and sometimes even wiser than others, particularly those of an optimistic nature. It forms the basis of a lot of humor and is a powerful force in our thinking.

But what does it do to our hearing? Does it make it more difficult to absorb the nutrients available through testimonies and other such positive input? It cannot help but do so.

### A Suspicious Mind

This is similar to a cynical mind. It questions the validity of experience, motivation and planning. It asks questions designed to uncover something negative rather than support the positive. It tends to drain the people subjected to its thoughts, making them question themselves in an unhelpful way. It has difficulty embracing revelation and tries to limit people to human reality.

When a child dreams of greatness, for instance, wise parents react with warmth and encouragement, thinking how they can help to see such dreams fulfilled. Reacting with suspicion will not only dampen that particular dream, it will inhibit the whole process of dreaming. No child dreams of being insignificant, but acceptance of insignificance is aided by suspicion. I have also heard it said that children have no difficulty believing in miracles, until someone teaches them otherwise.

Suspicion is a bad teacher for anyone of any age in the realms of the Kingdom of God. It is not to be confused with discernment.

### A Mind with Wrong Priorities

There are many sounds and voices fighting for our attention. Which ones do we spend the most time listening to?

In 1 Corinthians 6:12 the apostle Paul states, "'Everything is permissible for me'—but not everything is beneficial. 'Everything is permissible for me'—but I will not be mastered by anything."

I have mentioned how much I enjoy sports. Nowadays there are so many sporting events available through television, the Internet and local stadium seats that I could spend virtually my whole life listening to or watching sports. Is sport wrong? Certainly not. It is a great source of inspiration and relaxation. But where does it come in my priorities?

The same can be said of so many things. In developed countries, for instance, "retail therapy" (simply "shopping" to me!) has a huge pull on people's time and energy. Facebook, Twitter, computer games, television . . . all good things when used appropriately.

We need to make sure we have time to listen to what God is saying to us amid the clutter of other voices striving for our attention. We need to seek first the Kingdom of God.

These are some of the mindsets that can hinder us from absorbing into our beings the spiritual nourishment available to us. There are obviously others; perhaps you would like to consider what these might be.

## Consider Carefully

The Bible teaches that we are being transformed into the likeness of Jesus with ever-increasing glory (see 2 Corinthians 3:18). How does this transformation take place? We are "transformed by the renewing of [our] mind[s]" (Romans 12:2). In order for our minds to be transformed—to reject the things that hinder us and to receive spiritual nourishment—we need to unwrap malnutrition. We also need to remember the positive things that nourish us spiritually, rejoice in them and partake with gratitude.

We need to consider carefully how we listen.

## Unwrapping the Bonds

What shapes your thinking? Books? Television? Chat rooms? Your church? The Internet? Your friends?

Do you seem to have more "input" than "growth" in matters of the Kingdom?

Do you identify with any of the "mind" descriptions given in this chapter? What might God be leading you to do differently?

Can you think of any other mindsets that hinder you personally?

# 16

# UNWRAPPING FREEDOM

*Revealing the Purposes of Jesus*

If you could have a one-to-one conversation with any one person in the world, whom would you choose?

My choice would be Nelson Mandela, the man who led his country, South Africa, out of oppression into a new season of freedom and opportunity. He did it with courage and dignity. He is probably the man I admire the most—a true freedom fighter.

Yet when I was young, I believed the image portrayed to me of him as a bad man—a terrorist, a violent man. I was misinformed, and I have learned differently.

A few years ago Kim and I visited Robben Island. It was a moving experience and one that still affects me to this day. On that island, a short boat ride from Cape Town, Nelson Mandela was imprisoned for 18 years of his 27-year sentence. He was imprisoned for his part in trying to bring freedom to all South Africa's citizens.

We stood in his tiny cell where he passed countless hours. We visited the quarry where he had to crush rocks. Our tour guide had also been a prisoner there.

The message given on that island tour was of the triumph of dignity and courage over oppression; of hope overcoming despair; of a desire for equality for all men, women and children in South Africa. There was no talk of vengeance, but rather of reconciliation; the ex-prisoners of that place talk about Robben Island as the birthplace of democracy in South Africa. Nelson Mandela became the first president of the new South Africa founded on democracy and the desire for equality.

Nelson Mandela reminds me of Jesus.

Jesus is the ultimate freedom fighter. He proclaimed His mission in these words from Luke 4:

> "The Spirit of the Lord is on me, because he has anointed me to preach good news to the poor. He has sent me to proclaim freedom for the prisoners and recovery of sight for the blind, to release the oppressed, to proclaim the year of the Lord's favor."
>
> Luke 4:18–19

Jesus came to set people free:

- Free from sin, guilt and shame
- Free from demonic oppression
- Free from sickness
- Free to enjoy God's favor
- Free to be great in His Kingdom (see Matthew 11:11), to do His works and even greater works (see John 14:12)

Jesus gave His life to gain freedom for mankind. Freedom is at the heart of the Christian Gospel.

Such amazing freedom! It is the duty of the Church to fight for and guard this freedom with our lives, for a spiritual force has raged against it down the centuries.

## Entering the Battle

Let's look at the book of Galatians to help us in this godly fight.

> I am astonished that you are so quickly deserting the one who called you by the grace of Christ and are turning to a different gospel—which is really no gospel at all. Evidently some people are throwing you into confusion and are trying to pervert the gospel of Christ. But even if we or an angel from heaven should preach a gospel other than the one we preached to you, let him be eternally condemned! As we have already said, so now I say again: If anybody is preaching to you a gospel other than what you accepted, let him be eternally condemned!
>
> Galatians 1:6-9

Right at the beginning of this letter after the initial greeting, Paul launches into a defense of the true Gospel. He expresses astonishment that the Galatian church has deserted the truth of Christianity and is turning to another message, which is not the Good News at all! He talks about people throwing others into confusion and perverting the Good News of Jesus. This is strong language. He proclaims that anyone distorting the message of Christianity should be eternally condemned, such is the gravity of this matter.

What is at the root of this distortion of the Gospel? Paul talks about the desire to win the approval of men, about being a man-pleaser rather than a God-pleaser: "Am I now trying to win the approval of men, or of God? Or am I trying to please men? If I were still trying to please men, I would not be a servant of Christ" (Galatians 1:10). The fear of other people's disapproval is a powerful thing, as we shall see in this letter. The fear of man can ultimately stop you from serving God.

Then Paul wants people to know that the message he is preaching comes from heaven rather than any earthly source: "I want you to know, brothers, that the gospel I preached is not something that man made up. I did not receive it from any man, nor was I taught it; rather, I received it by revelation from Jesus Christ" (Galatians 1:11–12).

It is the message of heaven, and it is not to be distorted.

## Rejecting Legalism

As the basis for his teaching about freedom, Paul describes for the Galatians a meeting he had earlier with the church leaders in Jerusalem. That discussion involved the revelation he had been given about ministering to the Gentiles.

> Fourteen years later I went up again to Jerusalem, this time with Barnabas. I took Titus along also. I went in response to a revelation and set before them the gospel that I preach among the Gentiles. But I did this privately to those who seemed to be leaders, for fear that I was running or had run my race in vain.
>
> Galatians 2:1–2

The context for this passage can be found in Acts 14–15. Paul and Barnabas had just returned from their first missionary journey and given a report to their home church at Antioch about all that God had done through them. In particular, they talked about the door of faith being opened to the Gentiles (see Acts 14:26–27). The Good News of Jesus Christ was breaking out of the confines of reaching only the Jews—freedom was being proclaimed to the Gentiles as well.

During this exciting report, however, certain men arrived in Antioch from Judea and taught a different message. They contested the teaching that Gentiles could enter freely into salvation. They insisted that in addition to the saving grace of Jesus it was necessary for the Gentiles to earn their salvation through circumcision. These men were hitting at the heart of the Gospel. Paul and Barnabas got into a sharp dispute with them.

When you think about this thoroughly, not only were these men distorting the Christian message, they were effectively excluding women from salvation.

Confusion was brought upon the church in Antioch. But not only that —the Good News that was starting to break out across the world was being called into question.

In response to this, Paul and Barnabas were appointed by the church at Antioch along with some others to go to Jerusalem in order to consult with the church leaders there about the authenticity of the message they were preaching.

The outcome of this consultation was that the word of grace being preached by Paul and Barnabas was applauded by the apostles and elders in Jerusalem. They affirmed that neither circumcision nor any other work of man is necessary for salvation and freedom.

Notice Paul's explanation to the Galatians of how this matter came about in the first place: "This matter arose because some false brothers had infiltrated our ranks to spy on the freedom we have in Christ Jesus and to make us slaves" (Galatians 2:4).

Men who were making themselves out to be true representatives of Jesus and the church in Jerusalem had infiltrated the church in Antioch in order to spy on the freedom there and to try to return them to slavery. These people were known as

Judaisers—they were trying to retain an element of Jewish laws within the Christian message.

Adding any sort of human work as a necessary component of the message of salvation will result in slavery rather than freedom. I love the French translation of part of this verse, which says that these Judaisers "slid in among them as though on ice"—trying to infiltrate smoothly for the purpose of enslaving the people of God once again.

Paul and Barnabas, however, saw the vital importance of this issue. They did not give in to those men because the truth of the Gospel was at stake: "We did not give in to them for a moment, so that the truth of the gospel might remain with you" (Galatians 2:5). This is a vitally important issue. Any teaching that takes away from the freedom encompassed in the Gospel of Jesus Christ is to be resisted.

Legalism is not valid within Christianity; it restricts expression of our Christian faith. Legalism is opposed to the fundamental message of the Gospel.

So much teaching within Christianity has been directed at telling people how to behave rather than how to think. If we aim our discipleship at people's behavior, endeavoring to tell them what to do and what not to do, we will inevitably end up in legalism. The message of salvation through grace alone is so often quickly followed by a list of rules and regulations that you should follow now that you have "become a Christian." The message of freedom is distorted by a different message.

> As for those who seemed to be important—whatever they were makes no difference to me; God does not judge by external appearance—those men added nothing to my message. On the contrary, they saw that I had been entrusted with the task of preaching the gospel to the Gentiles, just as Peter had been to the Jews. For God, who was at work in the ministry of Peter as

an apostle to the Jews, was also at work in my ministry as an apostle to the Gentiles. James, Peter and John, those reputed to be pillars, gave me and Barnabas the right hand of fellowship when they recognized the grace given to me. They agreed that we should go to the Gentiles, and they to the Jews.

Galatians 2:6–9

Nothing was added to the message Paul was preaching. Paul and Barnabas were affirmed in their mission and message, and embraced by the other apostles as fellow workers. "All they asked was that we should continue to remember the poor, the very thing I was eager to do" (verse 10). The only request was that they continue to be considerate of one another, especially the poor, and Paul already had this in his heart.

## Even Strong Men Bend

Paul then tells an amazing story concerning the apostle Peter. Some time had passed (it is uncertain how long), and Peter arrived in Antioch.

When Peter came to Antioch, I opposed him to his face, because he was clearly in the wrong. Before certain men came from James, he used to eat with the Gentiles. But when they arrived, he began to draw back and separate himself from the Gentiles because he was afraid of those who belonged to the circumcision group.

Galatians 2:11–12

When Peter first arrived in Antioch, he ate with the Gentile believers, joining in with them at the meal table. He was living in freedom and demonstrating it. When some men arrived from Jerusalem, however, he separated himself from the Gentiles.

Why did he do such a thing?

The answer is the fear of man.

Peter was afraid of the "circumcision group" and what they would say about him. His reputation with them was more important to him than the truth of the Gospel!

Remember the story of Peter in Acts 10, when he had a vision of a sheet being lowered down from heaven? God had told him that nothing that His hand had made was unclean. This revelation enabled Peter to go to Cornelius' house, and the Gospel started to break out into the Gentile world.

Most of us would think that such an experience would be sufficient to keep us walking in the truth. But, no, the battle against spiritual freedom is a fierce and constant one. Even Peter was taken off track and succumbed to fear.

Not only that: "The other Jews joined him in his hypocrisy, so that by their hypocrisy even Barnabas was led astray" (Galatians 2:13). So powerful is this spiritual attack, and so seductive its appeal, that others joined Peter in replacing freedom with rules and fear. Even Barnabas, who had battled alongside Paul in the cause of the Gospel and freedom, was led astray.

Without diligence and careful spiritual awareness, we will let legalism infiltrate our lives. It appeals to our pride, convincing us that we can improve our relationship with God and increase His approval by our own works. It also plays on our desire to be approved of by others—even when it might mean compromising the truth of the Gospel.

Paul took matters in hand:

> When I saw that they were not acting in line with the truth of the gospel, I said to Peter in front of them all, "You are a Jew, yet you live like a Gentile and not like a Jew. How is it, then, that you force Gentiles to follow Jewish customs? We who are Jews by birth and not 'Gentile sinners' know that a man is not justified by observing the law, but by faith in Jesus Christ. So

we, too, have put our faith in Christ Jesus that we may be justified by faith in Christ and not by observing the law, because by observing the law no one will be justified."

Galatians 2:14–16

The truth of the Gospel is rooted in God's work, not ours. It is rooted in our faith in the works of God alone. It is rooted in freedom and not in fear.

## Set Free for Freedom's Sake

This foundation laid, Paul now has strong words for the Galatians who are also beginning to turn back from freedom and into law: "You foolish Galatians! Who has bewitched you? Before your very eyes Jesus Christ was clearly portrayed as crucified" (Galatians 3:1).

Strong language!

Who has bewitched you? In other words, who has introduced you to witchcraft? In biblical terms, witchcraft is a spiritual dynamic that takes control over people, enslaving them to fear and practices set against God. The Bible is adamant that we must have nothing to do with it. Equating the message of the Judaisers with witchcraft is a powerful image indeed.

Paul berates the Galatians for being foolish. He appeals to the work of the crucifixion of Jesus, clearly contrasting that with witchcraft. The work of Jesus produces freedom, not slavery to controlling spirits.

As we have noted, Paul seeks to address the issue with just one question: "I would like to learn just one thing from you: Did you receive the Spirit by observing the law, or by believing what you heard?" (Galatians 3:2).

Imagine: If you had just one question to ask in order to validate the truth of the Gospel, what would it be? Paul asks how they received the Holy Spirit—by works or by faith? The answer is that we can receive the Spirit only by faith in Jesus Christ, His perfect life, His death, His resurrection and His ascension back to heaven from where He sent the Holy Spirit.

Receiving the Spirit and continuing in the Spirit is possible by grace alone and is evidence of the truth of the Gospel. "Are you so foolish?" he asks. "After beginning with the Spirit, are you now trying to attain your goal by human effort?" (Galatians 3:3).

How foolish it is to think that having been born again by the Spirit, we can live our lives and try to attain our goals by relying on our own efforts rather than His enabling power! The activity of the Spirit is the fundamental validation of the Christian Gospel because it depends on the grace of God alone.

To give up freedom is to give up the Gospel. If we live without the dynamic activity of the Holy Spirit in our everyday lives, we cannot confirm the Gospel in all its fullness.

Second Corinthians 3:17 states this as well: "Now the Lord is the Spirit, and where the Spirit of the Lord is, there is freedom." The outcome of the presence of God is freedom.

Again, in Galatians 5:1 we read: "It is for freedom that Christ has set us free. Stand firm, then, and do not let yourselves be burdened again by a yoke of slavery." Jesus came to give us freedom. We are expected to fight to keep it and not let ourselves be enslaved once again.

*Freedom is a big thing.*

Freedom is in the heart and mind of God. God created humans with free will—with the ability to choose, even though this carries the risk of bad choices. Adam and Eve were created perfect and yet with the ability to choose to do wrong. Their freedom could bring damage to God's creation.

Why would God take such a risk?

Because of love.

Love requires freedom of choice; otherwise it is not true love. God is love, and God loves freedom.

Much of life has within it the balancing of benefit and risk. Every time I prescribe a medicine for one of my patients, I am calculating that the potential benefit of the medicine outweighs the risk of potential side effects. If the benefit is not greater than the risk, then I should not prescribe that medicine.

In God's calculation the benefits of freedom outweighed the potential consequences of poor choices.

So what sort of things do we need to guard ourselves against in order to maintain the freedom that Jesus has obtained for us, and not to allow ourselves back into slavery once again?

What can enslave us?

This subject deserves a book in its own right, but here are a few thoughts to get you thinking.

### Imposed Thought and Behavior

When we try to teach people what to think rather than how to think, we are in danger of enslaving them. The ability to think for oneself is vital to freedom. It is important we form our own opinions. It is important to think for ourselves, but not to think in isolation. Our thinking should be informed in a godly way—such as through Bible study, listening to others, listening to God, through experience. To try to force others to think exactly the same as I think takes away freedom.

I am not talking here about doctrines of the faith—beliefs such as the deity of Jesus, the Trinity, salvation through Christ alone. These are some of the "nonnegotiables." But there are other things where opinions can vary without threatening the fundamental truths of Christianity. Here is an example: Should a single person desire to get married, or is it better to stay single? You could argue for either case from the Bible. Trying to apply teaching without understanding the context can lead to problems that threaten freedom.

Along with forcing certain beliefs, it is also a threat to freedom to require certain behaviors. A friend of mine who was a youth worker in a church was "ordered" not to wear denim jeans because it was deemed inappropriate for his position within the church. A youth worker! He was threatened with disciplinary measures if he violated the church rule. His freedom to wear what he chose was curtailed, which undermined his message of freedom to the young people.

Philippians 4:8 gives some helpful instruction:

> Finally, brothers, whatever is true, whatever is noble, whatever is right, whatever is pure, whatever is lovely, whatever is admirable—if anything is excellent or praiseworthy—think about such things.

We need to help people know how to think in godly ways, so that they can make godly choices and live godly lives.

"But what about obedience?" I can hear you saying.

Obedience is crucial. The point is, however, that free people and slaves view obedience differently. Slaves obey because of fear. Free people choose to obey because of respect, honor and love.

"Through him and for his name's sake, we received grace and apostleship to call people from among all the Gentiles to the obedience that comes from faith" (Romans 1:5). There is a big difference between obedience that comes from faith and obedience that comes from fear. Faith is rooted in relationship, trust and respect. It flourishes in an atmosphere of freedom.

The Christian Gospel calls people into relationship with God, where obedience to Him is an outcome of knowing Him. It is sensible to follow the opinion and commands of someone who knows a lot more than oneself. In actual fact, it brings joy and peace.

As I mentioned, I have no trouble obeying my garage mechanic,

Mick, when he gives me advice, because I trust him and he knows more about cars than I do.

God knows all things and I trust Him. Obedience, then, is a joy not a duty or burden.

### Fear of Man

The fear of man will cause people to do things to gain the approval of man, just as the apostle Peter did.

The fear of disapproval by others is a potent enemy. It can cause us to conform to patterns of thought and behavior that erode our freedom. It can also stop us from voicing our own opinions and stop us from speaking the truth in love.

We need to disentangle the link in many people's minds between disagreement and disapproval. I can disagree without disapproving. It is an important distinction. It is vital in the guarding of freedom. Perfect love casts out all fear. God's perfect love is my security.

### Insecurity

Insecurity in people generally tries to find expression by seeking to "be in control" in some area of their lives. That might lead to certain patterns of behavior, which then become enslaving. Addictions commonly have this as one of their roots.

It can also lead them to seek to control others, thereby reducing the freedom of those people as well.

Insecurity can be dangerous for any one of us because we all have areas in our lives where we are vulnerable.

To guard against this we need to find our security in God and enjoy the freedom that Jesus has purchased for us. There are so many promises in the Bible that can help us in this regard. Jesus stated that He would never leave nor forsake us. Let us train our minds and guard ourselves against the attack of insecurity. Let us bathe in the love of God and find our security in Him.

### Pride

Pride will cause us to depend solely on our own thoughts; you can see the danger here. Although it is important to think for oneself, it is equally important not to think in isolation. We need to realize our own limitations. Pride will isolate our thinking apart from God and others and elevate us in our own minds in a way that can be destructive. True humility, rather than false humility, overcomes pride and attracts God's grace into our lives. True humility has honest recognition of our strengths and weaknesses.

### Ingratitude

A lack of thankfulness can enslave us in miserable thoughts and attitudes. It is no fun being around people who grumble all the time. Philippians 2:14 instructs us to do all things without complaining or arguing.

The Bible suggests an alternative: Be thankful in all circumstances. Think about the good stuff! This is one of the most powerful tools of freedom that I know personally in my life. Thank You, God, for thankfulness!

Much more could be said on this subject. I hope I have given you enough to start you thinking!

## Dreaming Big

Finally, in this chapter, I want to state that the freedom God offers is not just freedom from bad things such as sin and oppression, misery and anxiety. It is much bigger than that.

*It is the freedom to be . . .*

Please fill in the dots.

You have freedom to dream and enter into realms where God can do, through your life, more than you can ask or imagine.

You are invited by God into a life beyond imagining.

It is time to unwrap any bonds of slavery that are hindering us and enjoy the fullness of the freedom Jesus Christ has made available to us. Jesus has not just set us free from sin, guilt and shame; He has set us free to dream, to achieve amazing things, to be creative, to have fullness of joy and life, to enjoy the pleasures and resources of heaven.

Such amazing freedom!

## Unwrapping the Bonds

How does being a "man-pleaser" distort the spread of the Gospel message?

Why do you think the Judaisers wanted to keep Jewish laws active for believers?

Have you ever been subjected to legalism? Are you able to see how legalism violates the freedoms that Christ came to give you?

In what ways are you most susceptible to being controlled by others? In what way are you most likely to try to control others?

If you could be free in an area of your mind where you are bound, what would that freedom look like?

# 17

# UNWRAPPING THE FULLNESS OF GOD

## Revealing Your Unimaginable Potential

Her name is Cat (short for Catherine, I think).

She is a nurse and was attending a conference. A word of knowledge was given about people with bad knees, saying that God wanted to heal them. As she stood in response to this invitation, her knee, which had been problematical for some time, was healed instantly. The amazed, happy look on her face was beautiful to behold.

On the same evening, Julie, one of the students from our School of Supernatural Ministry, related the story of how she had received prayer, not long before, with regard to various problems she was having with her body, including being overweight. She awoke the morning after the prayer to find that her clothes no longer fit her—they were too large. She had lost a substantial amount of weight overnight, sufficient enough that she now wore a smaller size. As this story was related, a woman in the congregation thought to herself, *I would like that to happen to me!* So she asked Julie to pray for her. The next day she was ecstatic—she had lost seven pounds in weight overnight and needed some new clothes!

What is happening?

The power and love of God are flowing out to people.

This is possible because He is filling us from His fullness, even as we begin to grasp our unimaginable, unlimited potential in Him.

We see this concept in the book of Ephesians where we are told that we can be filled to the measure of all the fullness of God. That sounds good; somewhat difficult to comprehend, but nevertheless good.

Let's read from Ephesians 3:

> For this reason I kneel before the Father, from whom his whole family in heaven and on earth derives its name. I pray that out of his glorious riches he may strengthen you with power through his Spirit in your inner being, so that Christ may dwell in your hearts through faith. And I pray that you, being rooted and established in love, may have power, together with all the saints, to grasp how wide and long and high and deep is the love of Christ, and to know this love that surpasses knowledge—that you may be filled to the measure of all the fullness of God.
>
> Now to him who is able to do immeasurably more than all we ask or imagine, according to his power that is at work within us, to him be glory in the church and in Christ Jesus throughout all generations, for ever and ever! Amen.
>
> Ephesians 3:14–21

There it is in black and white—the fullness of God expressed in us.

This passage also states that God is able to do more than we could ask or imagine through His power at work in us. God wants us to be so full of His presence, His love and power that we simply overflow into the world around us. His measure is pressed down and overflowing.

On a number of occasions at North Kent Community Church, we have seen people healed of illnesses without any prayer, but simply by being in the environment. God "leaked out" onto them out of His fullness! Such stories are becoming more common in the Christian world. God's fullness in us is affecting the world in which we live.

So how does this come about? How can we realize such spiritual potential? If we read further on into the book of Ephesians I believe we find some answers.

> (What does "he ascended" mean except that he also descended to the lower, earthly regions? He who descended is the very one who ascended higher than all the heavens, in order to fill the whole universe.)
>
> It was he who gave some to be apostles, some to be prophets, some to be evangelists, and some to be pastors and teachers, to prepare God's people for works of service, so that the body of Christ may be built up until we all reach unity in the faith and in the knowledge of the Son of God and become mature, attaining to the whole measure of the fullness of Christ.
>
> Ephesians 4:9–13

In this passage, once again, we read about attaining to the whole measure of the fullness of Christ. In other words, this is something to which we can attain.

The context is that of Jesus having ascended to heaven after His death and resurrection, and from there giving gifts to the Church. Among the many gifts that Christ gives to the Body, Paul here mentions five: apostle, prophet, evangelist, pastor and teacher. Much has been said about the prominence of these "fivefold" gifts or ministries over the last number of years. It can be a confusing subject.

Who are they?

What do they do?

How do you recognize them?

What do these people offer in relation to your unrealized potential?

Please allow me to offer a few thoughts about this subject that you might find helpful.

These are not titles that can be attained; they are gifts from Christ that are given. They are not positions within a hierarchical structure, but functions to be outworked for the benefit of the whole Body of Christ, His Church. Their purpose is to equip all Christians to do the amazing things we read about in Ephesians 3 as we attain to the full measure of God.

I believe that our understanding of these five gifts is vitally important to that end. It is my belief that all five are aspects of Jesus Himself. By allowing our lives to be shaped by them we can be changed into His likeness.

Our primary model is Jesus.

Jesus is the apostle (see Hebrews 3:1).

Jesus is the Word of God—the prophet.

Jesus is the good teacher.

Jesus is the evangelist who came to proclaim the Good News.

Jesus is the Good Shepherd (pastor).

I believe it is important that we gain our primary understanding of these five ministries through the life of Jesus. This will then help us recognize these gifts in people so that we can benefit from the grace and anointing that such people carry in their lives.

I used to think these gifts (people) were rare and difficult to find, but I am changing my mind on this. I think I was looking through a lens or filter formed by a certain mindset that set such people up on a platform, giving them an elevated or superior status within Christianity. I think it is important that we move beyond such hierarchical thinking. I am now looking differently and trying to discern with the help of the Holy Spirit where He has placed His gifts within His Body, the Church. These people have been given authority from heaven for the benefit of all Christians so that they can equip believers to attain their full potential. They serve the Body of Christ so that the fullness of Christ can be expressed on the earth.

I hope that this chapter will help you and equip you to recognize such people more easily so that you can benefit from their input into your life.

The outcome of these ministries is that each Christian should have the opportunity to attain to the fullness of Christ. It would take another whole book to explore this subject in detail, so I know I am starting an exploration at this point and may leave you with lots of questions, but I do believe this is a vital component of Christianity that needs to be unwrapped more fully.

I believe that when trying to recognize people who have these gifts/callings, the first thing to look for is whether or not they produce an environment around them where other people start to exhibit the fruit of that particular gift. A prophet, for instance, will produce an environment where people start to hear God more confidently and understand when He is giving them words from heaven to pass on to someone else. The success of a prophet is not merely about how he or she prophesies, but about how many people are equipped to prophesy, also, by increased levels of faith in that particular realm.

An evangelist will produce evangelistic people.

A teacher will produce people able to think for themselves and teach others about God and His Kingdom.

A pastor will produce a healthy environment where people can grow spiritually, and where the members of a church have a healthy, supportive relationship with each other, encouraging and loving one another.

And what about apostles? In my experience this is where most confusion arises. What is an apostle? How do you recognize one? What does 1 Corinthians 12 mean when it says "first apostles"? I believe it is very important to unwrap this issue as it affects so many other issues, particularly how we can attain our full potential.

For this reason I will look at "apostles" in greater detail.

## What Does *Apostle* Mean?

I am not going to enter into a debate about whether or not the office of apostle exists today—my biblical understanding of this matter is that apostles are still a vital part of God's plan for His Church and for His Kingdom. We need them as much today as at any other point in history.

Let me ask you a question: When does the word *apostle* first appear in the Bible? I have asked many people this question and have had a variety of replies.

The answer is that the word *apostle* first appears in the gospels of Matthew, Mark and Luke. It is Jesus who uses it in the gospels for the first time.

> One of those days Jesus went out to a mountainside to pray, and spent the night praying to God. When morning came, he called his disciples to him and chose twelve of them, whom he also designated apostles.
>
> Luke 6:12–13

Having chosen His twelve disciples, He then describes what they are to be—apostles. To our Christian ears this is familiar wording. We are used to the idea of the twelve apostles who were with Jesus.

But how did it sound to those twelve?

It is generally agreed that the word *apostle* (*apostolos*, Greek) has at its root the meaning "to be a sent one." To my mind that is not a complete definition; rather, it raises a few more questions.

Sent from where and to where?

Sent by whom?

Sent for what purpose?

If I had asked one of my children to go to the supermarket to buy some milk they would have been sent, but that would not have made him or her an apostle!

In order to understand this in greater depth, we need to do some study. This takes a bit of investigation and digging, but I think the treasure is worth finding. I have personally found the most helpful source in this study to be Kittel's *Theological Dictionary of the New Testament* (not a bedtime read!). It is very much a reference book.

Summarizing from that source: The Greek word *apostolos* carries the meaning of "sent one." It was used in the Greek context of seafaring expeditions where people were sent with a purpose of discovery and colonization. In particular, it was used with reference to military expeditions and in this context became a political term. It could be used as an adjective (like "apostolic") particularly as a way of describing certain ships—an apostolic ship. It became used as a noun also for the same purpose to describe such a vessel. The word developed in its meaning to carry the sense of a fleet or naval expedition and further developed to designate the admiral or commander of such an expedition.

When the Greeks colonized other lands, they sought to establish not only their presence but also their culture. The apostle was sent to extend the boundaries of the Greek people and their culture. It appears that the word then found meaning in different people groups. It appears in the writings of Josephus, the Jewish-Romano historian, for example, where it carries the sense of an authorized emissary.

If we now apply this concept in the Roman context, we can understand more fully. When the Romans conquered lands, they sought to establish Roman culture and the benefits of Roman civilization in those lands. (Admittedly, their methods were harsh!) Roads, aqueducts, sanitation measures and other amazing engineering feats started to appear, and can still be seen to this day in many places across Europe and Northern Africa. The amazing *Pont du Gard* in southern France is a good example.

Not only did the Romans establish physical infrastructure, the opportunity to become a Roman citizen carried with it many benefits. The apostle Paul himself used the benefits of his Roman citizenship.

In the Roman context, the concept of apostle meant a military conquest with the aim of establishing Roman civilization and culture.

To the Jews this was something to be resisted. They were fiercely defensive of their own culture, resisting not only Roman but all Gentile influence upon them. Thus, when Jesus called His disciples "apostles," it may well have been a shock to them. It was a term that they would not necessarily welcome.

Why did Jesus use an essentially foreign word to describe those whom He was choosing to represent Him?

What did Jesus mean by the word *apostle* and what did it mean to be an apostle of Jesus?

## Jesus the Apostle

Jesus is "the apostle" so let's address certain questions regarding Him.

*Firstly, where was Jesus sent from and where was He sent to?*

Jesus was sent from heaven to the earth.

He was heaven's ambassador. The one sent "from above." He descended to the earth. He brought with Him the culture of heaven to be expressed on the earth—the Good News of the Kingdom of heaven. God walked on planet earth in bodily form, fully deity and fully humanity. Where He walked, heaven was expressed in the form of miracles, healings, deliverance, authority and freedom.

*Secondly, who sent Him?*

Jesus was sent by His Father.

He revealed His Father in heaven to the people of earth. He said that anyone who had seen Him had seen the Father. He and the Father are one. He came with the full blessing and authority of His Father.

*Thirdly, why was He sent?*

Jesus was sent to destroy all the works of the evil one. "The reason the Son of God appeared was to destroy the devil's work" (1 John 3:8).

That is a basic summary of why Jesus was sent. The works of the evil one have corrupted and damaged mankind and the creation we live in. Jesus came to restore all things, and in order to do so He had to destroy the bad things. Jesus was sent on a military mission to recapture planet earth and restore it to God's plans and purposes. It was essentially a spiritual mission, which overflowed into physical life.

Jesus destroyed the power of sin over us by His death on the cross. Jesus destroyed the power of death by His resurrection from the dead. Jesus' mission was to restore the Kingdom of heaven to the earth. An outcome of this was freedom, health and happiness.

Fourthly, what was the ultimate outcome of His mission?

The ultimate outcome for Jesus was His triumphant return to heaven having fully accomplished His mission on earth. Then

He poured out the Holy Spirit upon all mankind so that anyone with faith in Jesus could do the same works that He had done and even greater works!

The message of the grace of God and the Kingdom of God can now be fully preached with signs and wonders to confirm it. The full benefits of being citizens of heaven have been made available to all mankind.

I would summarize the apostolic nature of Jesus' ministry like this:

- Jesus came to reveal God to mankind in all His fullness.
- Jesus was the presence of God on earth.
- Jesus manifested the grace of God.
- Jesus did the works of God.

Now, regarding the twelve apostles, the instructions Jesus gave them indicate what they were called to do. Jesus was "re-producing" Himself in them.

> Jesus went up on a mountainside and called to him those he wanted, and they came to him. He appointed twelve—designating them apostles—that they might be with him and that he might send them out to preach and to have authority to drive out demons.
>
> Mark 3:13–15

Firstly, they were called to be with Jesus—personal relationship with God is the first priority.

They were sent from His presence to preach the Good News of the Kingdom.

They had authority over demons and sickness, enabling them to heal the sick, raise the dead, release the oppressed and bring freedom. In so doing they were destroying the works of the evil one and establishing the Kingdom of heaven on earth.

They took the culture of heaven with them and put it on display as the pearl of great price, which Jesus had talked about, so that people would want to come into full relationship with God as they saw His majesty displayed before them.

> When Jesus had called the Twelve together, he gave them power and authority to drive out all demons and to cure diseases, and he sent them out to preach the kingdom of God and to heal the sick. . . . When the apostles returned, they reported to Jesus what they had done. Then he took them with him and they withdrew by themselves to a town called Bethsaida.
>
> Luke 9:1–2, 10

The apostles went out from Jesus with power and authority. When they returned, they reported what they had done. They then spent more time with Jesus. This is a good pattern of behavior.

But what would happen when Jesus was no longer with them?

Jesus promised them something even better. He promised them the Holy Spirit.

The Holy Spirit is sent from heaven by Jesus and the Father. He is on an apostolic mission. He is continuing the same mission as Jesus.

- Holy Spirit comes to reveal God the Father and Jesus the Son to mankind in all their fullness.
- Holy Spirit is the presence of God on earth.
- Holy Spirit manifests the grace of God.
- Holy Spirit enables us to do the works of God.

After His resurrection Jesus told His disciples to wait for the Holy Spirit to come upon them before they embarked upon the mission He had given them. They would not be able to fulfill their mission without the Holy Spirit.

When we look at the book of Acts we get a good idea of how the apostles worked and what their priorities were: They proclaimed the Good News of the Kingdom of God, they performed miracles and they prayed for people to receive the Holy Spirit.

When they arrived somewhere new, their first question was usually to ask if people had received the Holy Spirit. (Samaria in Acts 8 and Ephesus in Acts 19 are good examples.)

- They performed miraculous signs and wonders.
- They fought fiercely the battle for grace against legalism, freedom against control.
- They taught and trained Christians to be apostolic in their own lives.
- They were dependent upon the Holy Spirit.

We looked earlier at the challenge that faced the church in Jerusalem—the Greek widows were being neglected in the distribution of food. The people to whom this work was delegated had to be known to be "full of the Holy Spirit and wisdom." Even the distribution of food should be infused with the activity of the Holy Spirit and heavenly wisdom. The apostles were training and equipping an apostolic church.

## Equipping the Church

In Ephesians 4:11–13 we read that the purpose of these five ministries is to equip the whole Body of Christ, His Church.

*Apostles* will produce an apostolic people, creating an apostolic environment.

*Prophets* will produce a prophetic people, creating a prophetic environment.

*Evangelists* will produce an evangelistic people, creating an evangelistic environment.

*Teachers* will create a learning environment and a well-taught people who are able to teach truth and explain it to others, helping to disciple the nations.

*Pastors* will produce a pastoral people, creating a pastoral environment.

All five ministries are needed if we are to attain to the full measure.

In 1 Corinthians 12 we read about spiritual gifts within the Body of Christ, every person having equal value and every Christian having an important part to play in God's purposes on the earth. Yet, an order is clearly given in verse 28: first apostles, second prophets, third teachers. . . .

There is order in God's purposes.

This is a functional order not a hierarchical one.

*First apostles* does not make them superior to others, as is clear from the chapter. It is saying that the part they play needs to be put in place first. It is an issue of foundations. The Church is to be built on the foundation of apostles and prophets with Jesus as the cornerstone.

When I went to medical school I started in the first year. Funnily enough, that was where we all started! It was not the pinnacle of our medical careers. Now, thirty years after graduating as doctors, those in my year group have developed to become specialists in many different fields of medicine. But we all started with the same foundations for our medical careers—anatomy, physiology, biochemistry, pathology, pharmacology, etc. The knowledge we gained and the practical aspects of our training enabled us to become the doctors we chose to be.

Apostles (and prophets) put in place foundations for Christian life that enable individuals and churches to pursue and fulfill the purposes of God. They enable people to be apostolic and prophetic in their everyday lives. Evangelists, teachers and pastors will be more effective working in such an environment.

## You Are "Apostolic"

If I were to ask you if you are apostolic, what would you say? You do not have to be an apostle to be apostolic, in the same way that you do not have to be an evangelist in order to be evangelistic. And yet we might hesitate to think we can be apostolic, because in our minds we might see this as part of a hierarchical structure of leadership, rather than an equipping concept whereby everyone attains to the fullness of Jesus.

So what does an apostle look like today? What does an apostle do? I suggest that an apostle looks like Jesus, particularly in regard to His apostolic characteristics. Similarly we could ask what it means for any Christian to be apostolic, since apostles will produce apostolic people.

I summarize these characteristics in four ways regarding apostles and apostolic people:

- Apostles will aim to reveal God to mankind in all His fullness.
- Apostles will value the presence of God above everything else.
- Apostles will teach, preach and demonstrate the grace of God.
- Apostles will do the works of the Kingdom of God in the same way that Jesus did.

Apostles will concentrate their thoughts and energies on revealing God to people, carrying His presence, preaching and demonstrating the grace of God and doing signs, wonders and miracles. They will have a *Kingdom-first* mentality and from the activity of the Kingdom of God they will lay foundational values in churches.

Second Corinthians 12:12 says that the things that mark out an apostle are signs, wonders and miracles. These things are dependent on God and cannot be produced by human effort. Apostles will create an environment where the activity and presence of the Holy Spirit are indispensable.

Apostles should create a culture that is full of the presence of God, the grace of God, the greater revelation of God.

*An apostolic environment will not be program-driven, but presence-centered.*

In an apostolic environment all the other spiritual gifts will be enabled to flourish to their full extent, and the Body of Christ will find full expression, its programs arising out of the hearts and minds of a people filled with the fullness of God, motivated by the love of God and enabled by the power and grace of God.

So how can you benefit from apostles, and the other gifts that God has placed among us? The Bible teaches that if we receive a prophet we will get a prophet's reward (see Matthew 10:41). I believe this applies to all the gifts, not just the prophets. It is important to be open to the concept that Jesus has given these gifts to His Church so that everyone can grow spiritually.

I would suggest that you ask God to help you recognize the gifts that He has placed among us and then open yourself up to receive their input so that you will get the spiritual reward. It is wonderful if you can have personal contact with such people, but you also have access through other means such as books, television, podcasts, CDs, DVDs, etc. I believe that if you earnestly seek for these gifts (of people) you will find them as God promised.

I have tried in this chapter, in a brief way, to help you recognize the gifts God has placed in people, so that you will benefit from the resources God has placed within them. I believe it is time to enjoy the full benefits of all the gifts Jesus has given, unwrapping any thinking and behavior that would hinder us in this regard, so that we can attain and enjoy the full measure of God.

## Unwrapping the Bonds

Do you believe that the power and love of God can flow out of you to others?

How would you describe the times when His fullness in you seems real?

How would you recognize heaven's authority invested in people in the form of apostles, prophets, evangelists, pastors and teachers?

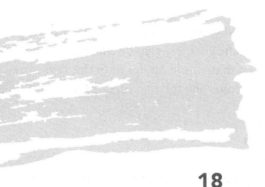

# 18

# UNWRAPPING THE FUTURE

## Revealing an Ongoing Adventure

One of the many Bible passages that has had a profound effect upon me over the years is the story of when Jesus returns to His hometown of Nazareth:

> Jesus left there and went to his hometown, accompanied by his disciples. When the Sabbath came, he began to teach in the synagogue, and many who heard him were amazed.
>
> "Where did this man get these things?" they asked. "What's this wisdom that has been given him, that he even does miracles! Isn't this the carpenter? Isn't this Mary's son and the brother of James, Joseph, Judas and Simon? Aren't his sisters here with us?" And they took offense at him.
>
> Jesus said to them, "Only in his hometown, among his relatives and in his own house is a prophet without honor." He could

not do any miracles there, except lay his hands on a few sick people and heal them. And he was amazed at their lack of faith.

Mark 6:1–6

This passage tells us that the people of Nazareth were initially amazed at Jesus' teaching and the miracles they were witnessing. But within a short time they took offense at Him. The outcome was that Jesus could not do any miracles there except lay His hands on a few sick people and heal them. (Most of us would settle for that!)

What happened?

The passage gives us some clues. The people experienced the teaching and miracles of Jesus, but then they processed these new experiences through the lenses of their previous knowledge and closed themselves to the idea of change.

They knew Jesus—He was the local carpenter, Mary's son. He was a hometown boy! He was familiar to them. In human terms they probably knew Him better than the people of any other town. They did not want to know this new Jesus, the one who worked miracles and taught with authority.

They took offense.

There is danger in familiarity—it can close our minds to new possibilities. It can also lead to the taking of offense.

If we allow our minds to be wedded to what we already know, we might not be open to new things. It is actually possible to so wrap our thinking with the familiar that we lose our freedom to think.

We should be open to the idea that we need to unwrap our thinking, taking off any restrictive ties of preconceived thought.

I am not suggesting that we abandon all that we have previously learned; that would be foolish. But not to be willing to embrace new things is equally foolish.

My training in medical school was thorough and rigorous, full of the latest knowledge and medical advances. But that was thirty years ago. The basic principles of the anatomy of the human body have not changed, but medical thinking has advanced, new medicines are available, new research has been conducted, new equipment has been developed and new techniques are available. Over thirty years I have needed to absorb these new things into my medical practice. Indeed, if I had not done so, I would no longer be fit to practice modern medicine.

Jesus presented Himself in a new way to His hometown, but they did not want to embrace what they saw. How sad Jesus must have felt that He could not do all that He wanted to do there! So many more people could have been healed if they had not been confined by familiarity.

## Unpredictable Outcomes

In this book I have attempted to look at issues that could be binding us in old ways of thinking and behavior, restricting us from living in the freedom that Jesus intends for us. Lazarus was raised from the dead, but he needed to be freed from the coverings that kept him from moving. New wine needs a new wineskin, but each new wineskin will age. The need to renew our minds is a lifelong discipline. Any established way of thinking or behaving can become restrictive if it is not open to new revelation, insights, discoveries and experiences.

Although God will never fit into a box, it is possible to form a box in our own minds in which we expect Him to fit. This has been true through the centuries, and it is still true today.

I like to think that I have a flexible mind. That is very different from a mind of compromise. I am not willing to compromise the truth, but I do recognize that I do not know all the truth. There is more for me to discover.

Late in 1993 a strange thing started to happen with me and in our church. We used to gather together regularly to worship, pray about issues and pray for each other. It was normal while praying for each other to have some sort of physical contact—a hand upon the shoulder and such like.

Suddenly, in one meeting, almost everyone I touched fell to the floor under the power of God. This continued in any meeting that I attended. I remember going to see a close friend of mine, who has been a spiritual adviser for many years, for his thoughts about this. His reply was not particularly helpful: "Don't worry; it probably won't last long." I was more interested in why it was happening rather than how long it might last!

It continued. In fact, it developed so that even if I simply touched people *without* praying for them, they fell to the floor, sometimes unable to get up again for some time. At the end of the meetings, when people wanted to go home, they started to avoid me!

I was intrigued. What was God doing? Was He saying something to me?

Other people in our church started to experience something similar though in a lesser measure. Church became interesting and unpredictable. We did not mind; we were happy and intrigued. When new people came, they experienced God in the same way.

I have mentioned that in early 1994 a visitation from God that originated in a small church in Toronto spread around the world. The anointing that God poured out there seemed to be transportable: People who visited Toronto returned home to see similar things occurring around them. Here in the U.K., gatherings sprang up all over the place so that people could receive what God was pouring out. I remember going to meetings where we were queuing for up to an hour to get in, such was the hunger and thirst for God.

All sorts of strange things happened—falling over, laughing, crying, much joy, people so intoxicated by the Holy Spirit that they found themselves incapable of walking. I remember going to one such meeting in which one of our church members fell to the ground, where he remained. He was happy to experience God. The problem was, however, that he wanted to stand up. He asked for help, but we could not get him up from the floor! We could not move him. It was as though he was stuck there with glue.

He started to get a bit uneasy about this, quite understandably, but I could not shift him. In the end I decided to ask Phil, one of our church members, to sit next to him. When Phil was touched by God he laughed continually, which was contagious. For the next hour and a half, the two of them laughed until eventually it was possible for the man to lift himself from the floor.

Many such strange things happened in our church. We had to open our minds to the new things that God was doing. We were not familiar with this stuff.

We started to hold meetings every Sunday evening for people to come and experience the presence of God. I recall one of our members "swimming" across the floor, breaststroke style if I remember rightly. When asked afterward what he had been doing, he said that the Lord had invited him to swim in the river of God.

Another time a woman laughed continuously for over an hour. She laughed so hard that little blemishes broke out on her face. When asked what had happened, she said that she had been repenting as God showed her how ridiculous some of her thinking was. Her mind was transformed.

We learned to judge things by the fruit they produced in people's lives and not by the external manifestations. People changed and drew closer to God. The box of our thinking was being challenged and broken down.

## Further Unboxing of My Thinking!

A little while later we had the privilege of hosting a team from the church where the Toronto Blessing started. We organized a weekend of meetings to learn and encounter God. In fact, we had the privilege of doing that on four separate occasions. On those weekends, our church got extremely blessed and enriched. God did many great things. By the time Sunday came around, the church was ready for pretty much anything God chose to do. And so was I—or so I thought!

One weekend, we were experiencing the presence and goodness of God in powerful ways. One of our members told me that she was planning to bring a friend with her to the next Sunday morning meeting. This friend did not yet have a personal relationship with God. His name was Martin. *Good,* I thought, with the expectation that this man would experience God.

On the next Sunday morning, the church was excited and expectant. I kept an eye out for Martin, and greeted and chatted with him when he arrived. It was his first time in any of our church meetings. He did not regard himself as having a relationship with God, but I hoped that was about to change. He took a seat about four rows behind mine.

I was "in charge" of the meeting, meaning that I opened it and stayed sensitive to the direction in which the Holy Spirit was leading so that we might better stay on track with Him. The musicians struck up the first song, and the congregation burst into exuberant worship. The atmosphere was full of God's presence.

At the end of the first song, as the sound of praise quieted some, one of our leaders, Mick, walked to the front and took hold of the microphone that we have available to help people be heard when they want to give a word of prophecy, testimony or other such to the congregation.

Mick started to exhort the people.

"I am feeling passionate!" he started.

*Good,* I thought.

"God is passionate for us," he continued.

*Yes, excellent,* I thought, my mind focused on the effect of such words on the congregation.

"God wants us to be passionate for Him," Mick said to the people.

I was in full agreement.

"God wants us to show how passionate we are," he said.

I was nodding my head. I love passionate worship.

Mick was in full swing now, about to deliver the final part of his exhortation to the congregation.

"I think God wants us to kiss each other!"

My mind immediately went into overdrive. *No!* formed in my head. I was "in charge" of the meeting, and it was my duty to see that things progressed "properly." Foremost in my thinking were our visitors, of whom there were many that day, and in particular Martin, who had come for the first time and was sitting four rows behind me.

What would he be thinking? How would this affect him?

I was trying to think of a way of extracting us from this "predicament." It is reasonable to say that our meetings are open and free, but I was not sure we could be that free. How could I say no and carry on with the meeting? It is amazing how many thoughts can pass through your mind in a few seconds!

I had thought I was open to God's promptings, but was this God? And was I ready? Had I formed a box in my thinking that could limit expectation of what God could do and what we were ready for? After all, the Bible instructs us to "greet one another with a holy kiss" (Romans 16:16).

To people from some nations this might have been less of an issue, but I am English and most of our congregation was

English. Kissing in public is not really something we are comfortable with.

While my mind sped through the options and the issues, Mick got ready for action! Without hesitation he put down the microphone and headed straight for me. He took my face in his hands, and landed a big kiss on my cheek. With this, the congregation decided it was okay, and that it was time to join in! They started kissing each other and, as they did, the power of God fell upon people in an extraordinary manner. People fell to the floor; there was laughter, spontaneous praise, uncontainable joy. It was holy chaos. This continued for about twenty minutes. God had broken out of the box (not that He ever fits into one!).

But my boxed thinking had not been broken. I sat on my chair worrying! I was not enjoying the party. I was not joining in—not because I thought it was wrong, but because I was worrying about Martin.

God has not given us a spirit of fear, and He tells us not to be anxious about anything; I was not in the right spirit at that moment. The limitations of my thinking were being exposed, but, to my mind, they were justified.

I do not remember the rest of the meeting apart from the fact that all I wanted to do was check on Martin. I had not dared look in his direction for fear of seeing that he was unhappy and uncomfortable. At the end of the meeting I made my way toward him and somewhat awkwardly started a conversation.

"How did you like the meeting?" I asked.

"Very friendly," he replied. (I tried to hide my surprise.)

"I realized that you like kissing each other, so I decided to join in."

He had done better than I had!

He explained further. "I turned to the lady next to me, whom I have never met, and gave her a kiss on the cheek. She immediately fell to the floor and stayed there for twenty minutes."

227

My face must have been an absolute picture. You could have knocked me over with a feather.

He continued, "I have never had that effect on a woman before!"

Martin liked our church!

He had experienced God's touch alongside human love and friendship. He kept coming, and a few weeks later I prayed with him as he committed his life to Jesus.

How different the outcome might have been if I had managed to have my way in that meeting, rather than God's will being done! It really is better if God is in charge of our meetings. God is able to work outside the boundaries of our thoughts and imaginations. He is not limited to our way of thinking.

More recently, some friends of mine were talking to a man who was running a market stall in our local town. They asked him if he had any need they could pray for, in particular health problems. He could not think of anything he needed, but his elderly grandmother had a problem with her shoulder. My friends decided to pray for the man so that he could go home and pray for his grandmother, which he did, and she was healed.

God does things that surprise us.

When He does we have to be careful not to take offense or miss the opportunity presented to us. We have to beware being so familiar with Jesus that we do not recognize when He wants to do something new. We need to unwrap any ties that familiarity might place around us.

## The Logical Conclusion

During this book I have tried to unwrap aspects of our thinking and expectation that stop us from fully expressing the life God has given to us. God does not fit inside any box. It is easy, however, to form a box in our minds that establishes boundaries in which we expect God to express Himself.

The ability to be transformed by the renewing of our minds is something we need to maintain throughout life. It is relatively easy to recognize the need to change some old practices and old ways of thinking, but one of the greatest challenges can lie in the area of more recent advances and experiences. All too commonly, new revelation and experience will become a formula by which we define ourselves, rather than a stimulus to continued learning and development. We might start to carry new labels, have new practices and develop new structures that in themselves are good, but if they become rigid and immovable they will develop into new restrictions.

We need to be dependent continually on the Holy Spirit, rather than our own methods and efforts.

Having unwrapped Lazarus, it would be foolish to wrap him up again.

## Unwrapping the Bonds

Is there some "new thing" that God is nudging you to embrace?

What manifestations of the Holy Spirit might you be afraid of? Why?

What is the hardest thing that God might ask you to do?

Can you let Him direct the ongoing adventure that is your life?

# CONCLUSION

This is the first book I have written, and as I was writing a thought came to mind: *How do you finish a book such as this?*

In one sense it is an unfinished work, since there is always more to say and learn. Many questions will remain incompletely answered; indeed, I would not be surprised if you have even more questions at the end than you had at the beginning!

You might not agree with all that you have read, and that is okay with me, since I value your ability to disagree without disapproving. Also, there can be more than one way to look at things; there can be more than one correct way of approaching a matter.

Above all, however, I hope that I have gotten you thinking. If so, I will have succeeded in what I set out to do. I aim to teach people how to think rather than what to think, as I believe this is the best route toward maturity. So please think these things through for yourself, study the Bible, ask Holy Spirit to lead you into all truth and talk with friends whose opinions you respect.

Lazarus was raised from the dead, but he was not completely free until he was unwrapped. He needed to be unwrapped to live his life to the fullest. My hope is that you will discover more and more the riches of the life God has given you.

God offers us new life through being born again by the Holy Spirit—an abundant life filled with His goodness, love and power. It is a life that needs to be developed. Sometimes it can get entangled and restricted. My aim is that any unhelpful thought patterns and behaviors can be brought to light and then unwrapped from our lives, so that we can enjoy the fullness of the life that God has given to us. Not only that, but also that our lives will be a demonstration of the Kingdom of heaven to others so that they can see this "pearl of great price" and choose to purchase it themselves with their own lives.

Jesus is amazing. I want all the world to know Him.

I have tried to include the issues that I believe have high priority in this process of unwrapping. Doubtless there are things not mentioned in this book, but I hope I have given you a framework for thinking now and in the future.

In our church and our School of Supernatural Ministry we have a framework based on "3 I's":

Identity

Intimacy

Impact

We believe that understanding the identity of God and our God-given identities as His sons and daughters enables us to develop intimate relationships with Him. As these relationships grow, the fruit of the Spirit will grow in our lives, spiritual gifts will be released and we will naturally have an impact on the world around us.

My Christian life has developed enormously over the last five years. I have benefitted from being unwrapped myself and now live in a level of freedom that I did not realize was possible previously. It has been exciting and challenging.

I look forward to continuing my adventure of faith, confident that God wants to enable me to experience more of Him and be filled to the measure of all the fullness of God. I want this to be the experience of others as well. In fact, I am confident that future generations will experience more of God than this generation during their earthly lives—not because we are somehow lacking, but because God is infinite and eternal and there is no end to the discovery of His nature. Our journey will continue throughout eternity. What a beautiful thought!

I hope this book will continue to help you enjoy the life God has given to you and also help you on your journey into His fullness.

Please allow me to finish by praying for you using two passages from the Bible:

> I keep asking that the God of our Lord Jesus Christ, the glorious Father, may give you the Spirit of wisdom and revelation, so that you may know him better. I pray also that the eyes of your heart may be enlightened in order that you may know the hope to which he has called you, the riches of his glorious inheritance in the saints, and his incomparably great power for us who believe.
>
> Ephesians 1:17–19

> For this reason I kneel before the Father, from whom his whole family in heaven and on earth derives its name. I pray that out of his glorious riches he may strengthen you with power through his Spirit in your inner being, so that Christ may dwell in your hearts through faith. And I pray that you, being rooted and established in love, may have power, together with all the saints, to grasp how wide and long and high and deep is the love of Christ, and

to know this love that surpasses knowledge—that you may be filled to the measure of all the fullness of God.

Now to him who is able to do immeasurably more than all we ask or imagine, according to his power that is at work within us, to him be glory in the church and in Christ Jesus throughout all generations, for ever and ever! Amen.

Ephesians 3:14–21

Pete Carter is a medical doctor and church leader. Since becoming a Christian in his teen years, he has pursued the full reality of Christianity being outworked in his daily life. He is part of the senior leadership team of North Kent Community Church, a vibrant church based in Gravesend and New Ash Green in the United Kingdom. He continues to work as a doctor, and has a passion to see good medical practice and Christian healing stand side by side to benefit those who are sick. To this end he has established a healing center based at the church. Over the years Pete has seen many miracles happen in Jesus' name, some of which are recounted in this book.

Pete is a popular speaker at conferences and other events and is part of the teaching staff of the School of Supernatural Ministry at North Kent Community Church. He has traveled to many different nations and loves to enrich lives wherever he goes. If you ask Pete for his job description, he will say, "To bring hope wherever I am."

Pete is also a family man and takes great delight in this aspect of life. He has been married to Kim for more than thirty years. They both maintain a youthful zeal for life and thoroughly enjoy being parents and grandparents.

Pete is also a sports fanatic. One of his dreams is to still be playing squash at the age of seventy—which is a few years off yet! Attending the London Olympic Games with his family was a highlight to be remembered.

More details about Pete and North Kent Community Church can be found at www.nkcc.org.uk or www.unwrappinglazarus .com.